Inspirational Thoughts from Afar

from

The Little Scribe

First published in Great Britain by UPSO Ltd in 2006

All paper used in the printing of this book has been made from wood grown in managed, sustainable forests.

ISBN13: 978-1-907172-37-3

Printed and bound in the UK
Pen Press is an imprint of Indepenpress Publishing Limited
25 Eastern Place
Brighton
BN2 1GJ
A catalogue record of this book is available from the British Library

Other titles by the author:

The Little Scribe
More Thoughts from the Little Scribe
Further Thoughts from the Little Scribe
An Anthology of Thoughts from the Little Scribe
The Pathway to Inner Thoughts from the Little Scribe
Precious Thoughts from The Little Scribe
Thoughts of Comfort and Guidance from the Little Scribe
Know Thyself and Know Thy God, Final Thoughts from the Little Scribe

Inspirational Thoughts from Afar

from

The Little Scribe

by

Ron Bateman

A few words of explanation regarding the writing in this little volume:

In March 2000, my lifelong friend and companion died, and soon afterwards I was "prompted" to sit down and write, and what I wrote surprised me. I was "told" via these writings that they would come from brothers who belong to what is known as "The White Brotherhood" and that they would work through Brian, (my companion), and that I was to be the last link in the chain as it were, for their teachings. I am often wakened in the early hours and I go to my study and write quickly for about an hour or so, then I go back to bed and sleep. When I get up in the morning I read what has been written and then record it on a cassette; then I listen to, and hopefully learn from, what has been written. I am just the Scribe and can take no credit for what is written, but I feel very privileged to be part of this on-going teaching, and am very grateful to my brothers and Brian.
To those of you who have read this little volume I hope the words of comfort have helped you, and to those who are searching I trust you have found what you were looking for. May the blessings of the One on high be with you now and always.

I dedicate this book to Brian who is the inspiration for it, and to Irene, without whose help and encouragement this book could not have been written.

Thank you.

Ron Bateman

"The Little Scribe"

Chapter 1

May 29th 2003 12.30 a.m.

THINK! THINK! THINK!

You often wonder about what awaits you when it is your turn to leave this mortal body and put on your new one of Translucent Light. For it is translucent, and yet it is still your known body! Bewildering? Do not wonder for your physical body is but a temporary one while you reside upon this lower plane of existence. You need that heavier vehicle for your planet is one of dense substance, and where we are, and where one day you too will be is one of finer and lighter "vibrations". Though even those words cannot describe adequately what "our" worlds are like!

Try to imagine this your earthplane on the brightest and loveliest of days when all around is tranquil and harmonious, well now think of that sphere a hundred times more beautiful in every way. The "air" nothing like yours, for ours is not only our life force but is also our nectar, all around us is complete harmony, so that there is nothing to jar our sensibilities. All is true and good but do not be mislead into believing that we do nothing but float around, blissfully, unaware of our surroundings. Far from it, for all is "life vibrating" and so we vibrate in unison with it. We work, we talk, we act, just as you do upon your dark little sphere! For to us it appears that way, though to you it appears light, but your light is nothing compared to ours!!!

Once you step out of and beyond your earths vibrations, you are released, and begin to not only live, but enjoy your new found freedom, no more restrictions either of the body or the mind and that part is most important, for it is that "organ" that requires more and more stimulation if it is to grow and become what it has always been intended to be a beacon of light. For we when we become what you term "a spirit" throw off all earthly forms and vibrations that have restricted not only our body but also our Thinking for it is the thinking that is the impetus we need to further us on our upward path to complete realization, which we must add does not take place immediately you leave this earthly shell.

You still have many more lives to live and enjoy on your way back to the Source of all creation. So you see, there is no hurrying needed, the "Source" will always be there, always has been and always will be!

You will have many more "incarnations" if that is what you wish to call your new and various lives, and each one different from the last, more knowledge attained and stored within that computer like organ that you upon earth call your "mind". For it is an "organ", though it cannot be seen as such for it is a form of realization an understanding of what it is that inhabits those various bodies or cloaks of disguise that you "put on". You will then think "put on" does that mean that I am something that requires a garment to clothe whatever it is that I am?? And the answer little friend is Yes!! But not in the sense of a gross form of matter. Here you are all light, and formless, and yet you still remain a viewed likeness of who you really are!! Confusing? Well I will try and explain. The real you, is not the one that you have been used to while dwelling upon earth, that is only a temporary, biological form of existence, which is used to guide the inner being on it's sojurn upon your earth. For wherever you are in the many Universes, you always require a "form of reference", do you understand what is being told you? A "form of reference" also denotes that gross body you have just left behind!

On all "spheres" or rather states of awareness you need a "reference" and why? Because you are viewed and also do the viewing, and so you need something positive to behold, do you not? You cannot converse with what is not there can you? You begin to understand little person?

We are "persons" too, but that word is only for you to understand, for we are not like "persons" as you think of as "person". We are "made up" as it were of light, and electrical impulses, which in turn forms itself into what we "wish" or rather Think and so we become what it is that we feel is needed for as long as we deem necessary. But our true form is to you an illusion, though to us a reality, and will be to you as well one day!! All "spheres" or rather states of perception are "made up" of different substances or vibration and so "we" are able to use that substance matter to create who and what we are!!!!

For here, we are what we are and yet we are also what we observe!!! We not only vibrate as an "entity" but also a living throbbing realization of where we are!! Simply put, we are part of the sphere or planet that we inhabit! So that what affects one, affects All. Difficult perhaps for you to grasp, but think of where you are at present, are you not a part of all that is around you? What you do not only affects you but also those with whom you come into contact, also your surroundings, have you not thought of them before? What you do, or think has an effect, not only of yourself but the immediate members of your community, and that in turn should also be all of humanity!!! But that perception is lacking and so you create your own disharmony upon your planet!

In "time" this will be understood and worked upon, and then you will find a whole new life opening up before you. But we do not see that happening yet, or for some "time" to come. But it Will! It Will! For it has been decreed. You begin to wonder how does all this affect you personally? Well it is to stimulate your "thinking cells" to find our just who you really are, and yet you will not know that for a long, long time to come!! We never really know who we really are. We think we do, and then something happens which alters our whole thought process. We are always changing, not only our "being" but also our "Mind perception".

That illusive little organ that is there but not perceived!!! You have wondered we know as to what and who it is that motivates you, not only upon the earth plane but beyond! Many people would say "Your spirit" but even that requires an animator does it not? We don't just Be we have to be motivated to Be, do we not? And so there has to be a "motivator" and what do you imagine is "that"!!! Think little friend Think and you know the answer for you have just written it!!!!

We feel that you have had sufficient stimuli for this sitting, more will be given to you at another time, and please remember this is not only for you, but for others who are also seeking more knowledge and understanding of the Why!!!!

We bid you Farewell, for that is the correct way to finish this discourse we are told.

Farewell little person of the earth, and thank you.

Chapter 2

June 3rd 2003 Morning

THE SO CALLED AFTER LIFE!

Dear Brother in Christ Consciousness we welcome you once again. Shall we commence with The "after life" and what it is that you people upon the earth think about it? For many of you have strange and varied ideas of what it is like, please believe us when we tell you it is nothing like what you imagine it to be!!! For there are numerous so called "Spheres" that go to make up your so called "After life", a most peculiar expression, when we who dwell there would hardly call it an "After Life", for that implies something that is more akin to death than life when the complete opposite is True for life really does mean what that word implies, for here life is not only lived to the full, but it is full of life!!!

You don't just cease living because you leave the earth bound body behind you, an outworn carcass that is ready to disintegrate and return to dust where it belongs!! Your real body has now been released and can resume it's natural habitat namely one of the many worlds that it has previously dwelt upon, yes and lived upon!!! Does that make you wonder? You think to yourself, well if I've dwelt upon these worlds before, why should I get this feeling of apprehension at returning to them? That is merely the physical getting in the way of the so-called spiritual, and here we are talking in terms of "bodies", which is for your understanding. For the word "body" is to put you as ease, for it is something that you can recognise. If we were to say Translucent light waves you would have no idea of what it is we are describing, and yet dear friends, that is exactly what we are all made up of! Only here, we are all the same whereas upon earth your substances are dense and dark and so cannot be observed as light emanations and yet you are, and can be seen by certain persons gifted with that organ of inner sight!!!

Once you have thrown off that garment from earth then you can be seen as you really are a "translucent being" of pulsating and vibrant life form! Capable of many things but not we hasten to add immediately you transfer to the side of life you call Spirit!!

You see all things to do with your new expectation of the new life form, have to be taught and learnt!! It will be familiar to some, but to others it will no doubt seem strange and wonderful and somewhat beyond their present comprehension! But then that is all taken into consideration when we deal with the new body of light!! Do not worry for you do not automatically become bodies of light, at least not yet to the "physical eye as it were".

Here we consider ourselves and all things as "physical" for upon this plane we endeavour to help you to feel "at home! And not overawed by your surroundings, and so all is "scaled down" to how you feel comfortable with!! This goes not only for surroundings but also for the inhabitants of those surroundings! In time when you have adjusted to these new surroundings you will be able to perceive them as they really are, you see, little friends, not all things seen are what they appear to be!!! Difficult for you to quite understand we know, but it is a reality believe us when we tell you that it is so! For even upon your earth you know yourself that what the eye perceives is not always what lies underneath out of sight! Think upon that!!!

So now we can begin to deal with you as you now know who you are, that is when you have become "adjusted". But even then, you are still not the one who you think you are!!! You are aware now of others that you are, and yet not quite sure of, for you feel, "who am I really?" if there are others of me that exist elsewhere!!! Do not be alarmed for even when you dwelt upon earth you were aware to some extant of the other you, namely the one you call "Spirit", so you see you already had two "bodies" to use, even if you were not always aware of that other one!!! It seems that with age you begin to become aware that there is more to you than just your physical shell that you have to inhabit as a cloak of protection from earth's dense atmosphere!!! And so after shedding that one, you are now free to "put on" as it were, another cloak, to vibrate within, so that that "cloak" can take on the appearance of what you wish to be both observed and known by!!! Think upon that!! We are all capable of changing our "appearance" to suit the surroundings! No, dear friend, we don't just keep changing our appearance for the fun of it, it has to be for a specific purpose! All this "effort" has to be learnt. You will have keen and sympathetic "teachers" who will be able to instruct you on these procedures, just like going back to school again, only this time the theory is put into practice to help fit you for your lives to come!!! You notice we have said lives, for this first one that you have embarked upon is only one of very many, another form of training ground as your earth one was while you were upon it!!!

You will adjust, and I'm sure quite quickly for you, that is those who are open minded about these matters are already learning to adjust to the "other side" of your present existence!! You are the thinkers of this world of yours, so go one thinking and re-adjusting yourselves to the ever changing circumstances, and here we talk of the ones inside you, not the outward ones that affect the body!!! Your Mind is the governing and driving force that enables you to begin to see, what this life of yours is all about!! Clear your mind of all unnecessary baggage, cast aside your outgrown thoughts, and start afresh!! You are with our help quite capable, far more than you realize and as you learn to progress in Thought so you will progress within the body, and what seems like a coincidence is in reality not, but a well thought out plan of action instigated by the one who dwells within you!!!

We feel that that is a good note to finish on, and we will continue with this discussion at our next sitting. So until then dear friends we bid you farewell. Our next talk will take you further in your search for the Truth!!

Farewell to one and all Farewell, and to you little scribe blessings from the One on High be upon and within you, now and forever. Farewell. Farewell.

Chapter 3

November 16th 2003 1.50 a.m.

KNOW THYSELF

In tonight's discussion we will start with the words, "Seek and Ye shall find, knock, and the door shall be opened unto you"!!! Those words, convey much if one stops to analyse their meaning! "Seek and ye shall find"! And what is it that we must seek and then find? Have you thought that one out dear friend? The answer is Yourself!!! For in all your searching, the reasons for living and then dying and then being re-born, all things that are mysteries that need explaining and yet the solution is so simple! Look within yourself!! There you will discover what you are looking for! The answer to what life is all about is knowing thyself and when you do, then you are on the way to knowing who you really are! No, not this outward shell that is your home while you tarry upon the earth sphere, but the hidden You, the real one that knows who and what it is, a part of the Divinity that you call upon as God, that is the real you and when your search is over then and only then will you begin to know that, which has been to you unknowable!!! Your God if you have not discovered is You! But you are just a small part of that Supreme One, just a part which never the less is a part that goes to make up the whole!!! We are all those small parts, and when we accept that fact as a reality and begin to live as part of that truth, then we can really say that we have found the path back to the Divine Source from which we have originated from!

God, as you wish to call your source of life giving energy is not some far off unseen, unknown creature or myth from the past! But is the today's source of all inspiration that dwells within all of us! All living breathing creations of the Divine source of creative activity!! We are as it were like a bundle of wires, all mixed up together each wire a mental source of energy, unravel those wires and you will find that they will come together and emerge as pure pure Spirit essence! Alive, vibrating, part of the whole, that is why what we do, affects others, as they in their turn affect us!!! We cannot escape that fact, for it is a fact, a fact of Life itself! When we begin to accept that, then we can begin to see the mystery of life unravelling and see it in all its simplicity. Life, and Love, one and the same, given freely by the Almighty One to all of His children without distinction!!! When you look upon your brother or sister you are not only looking upon yourself but also your God in His manifested glory. For this living organism is glorious is it not? To be full of the life force that is all around us and yes within us also! We belong to each other as we belong to "Him". The Unknowable Source of All Creation. Look around you and marvel at what you can see and observe, and what you see is just a fraction of what Creation is all about! When Mankind sees in another human being a reflection of not only himself but His God also and lives the life of unselfishness then you will begin to see what the word Heaven is supposed to represent! Harmony, Unity, each soul a part of the whole, separate yes, but also belonging to the One who is our Creator and Source of all life! Seek and you will find that you are the answer that you are seeking!

"Knock and the door shall be opened unto thee". The "door" is the knowledge that has been given to those who seek, it is there on the other side of that door, waiting to be discovered, put the key in the lock, turn the handle and open the door and reveal the sunlight of understanding that will flood through and illumine your whole self. That is the one that dwells within the mortal body that encases the Spirit Essence of the Almighty, the real you. It is only you who can unlock this door! You are the key, and you alone!! We each have our own door to unlock, and go through, no one can do this for us, it is up to us, you know, that on the other side of that door lies eternity!! The real life that is waiting to be lived. You can call that door what you like, it can be an awakening it can also be a re-newing of the true life that has been hidden from the mortal body while it remains upon the earth! Some may call it the door of death, for to die in the body is to live in the Spirit, it is released from its bodage and is free once again. Go through that door and close it behind you, you have no need to look back once the door has shut. You are now on the side that beckons you to your new life, the one you left behind you, while you visited upon the earth, but which is now your permanent home, from which the way is forever forward and upward. Never more to return to the plane where you have learnt your lessons of life!! Life is for living and the true living of it brings you ever nearer to your Creator, that part of you that knows itself as God made manifest. You have found the reason of what life is for and what it is all about. You know who you are it may have taken you many so called lifetimes, but eventually you will know the reason for all of those lessons that had to be learnt, that bring you ultimately back to where you began this long, long, journey of discovery!! We all take this journey, and in the journeying we discover who we really are, and when we have made that discovery then we are re-united once more with the Creative Source of all Life and our life's journey has ended. Eternity beckons us, we are home, we are safe, we are back where we belong!!

Farewell dear friends, Farewell, keep on searching and you will be rewarded and the reward is knowing Yourself and knowing who you are. Farewell little Brother scribe, Farewell.

Chapter 4

November 17th 2003 2.30 a.m.

WHERE IS HEAVEN?

Dear friend and fellow Brother in Christ, we bid you welcome.

Cease your worrying regarding your thoughts, they will not intrude upon ours dear friend, so let your pen hand do its work, we shall now begin!! Life at times can seem very bewildering, we think that we are in control of it and all of a sudden we find ourselves in a position where we find we have lost that control, circumstances have arisen that seem to have taken over that authority! Yet when perhaps later, even years later and we look back at life we find that the period that we went through was planed and was all part of the overall scheme of things, we lost control and yet somehow it didn't matter for things turned out to our advantage after all!! No wonder life seems very perplexing, but that is what life is all about! We cannot always see the way ahead as we would like to, and yet it does work out doesn't it? There are times when we feel that there is someone else or something else that is guiding not only our very thoughts but our actions as well!!! And who or what is this guiding force? Can it be our inner self? The one we call our Spirit or is it an outside influence that has taken over? Perhaps it is a little of both of those thoughts! We gradually learn, and as life progresses we find that we accept it as it unfolds, not always can we see the picture that is being created, it is only in retrospect that that occurs! That is Life!, all part of our education for the future journey that will take us through not only many lives upon the earth plane but also in the World to come, the one you call the Spirit one!!!

That one, that is the eternal one that takes us back to the source of all Creation!! Sounds very grand and perhaps a little daunting doesn't it? But it is all part of the overall scheme of what is called cosmic evolution. We are all a part of this scheme of things, even when we can't quite understand where it is leading us to!! But then that is the wonderment of it all! If everything was shall we say cut and dried, there would be no incentive to try and progress would there? It is this very uncertainty of life that gives us the impetus to strive, to grow, to mature, to become what God in His wisdom has envisaged for us!! It is this growing up that is bringing us closer to that Divinity, even if we do not always see it in that light!! If we can learn to accept that we are, not only, a part of God, but also a child of God then we can start to live as "He" wants us to. How we react to what we call situations is all apart of our learning about our inner selves, the real governing part of us, in other words the God part of us, the part that knows!!! If we can bring that part of us to the fore and not keep it in the background as is so often the case, we would find that life makes so much more sense, than we sometimes give it credit for!! Once we learn to give ourselves to this Divine spark that dwells within us all we will find not only peace and contentment but we will also see that the path we are treading is the one that is leading us back to where we really belong, in the bosom of the Creator, Heaven if you like to call it that, for after all that is what we are told is where our life is leading us to isn't it? But Heaven need not be a place but an acceptance of who and where we are. We originate from the Divine source that we call God, we are part of that life force and when we return to it we bring with us an accumulation of what we have learnt, it is not wasted, for we are an essential part of the life force that is forever creating. Life goes on in all of its various aspects and we are part of that creativity, we do matter, for it is through us that those of the future generation have their being!!!

So if we can learn to live in a manner that can be termed a form of service to the Almighty which in reality is being of service to our fellow man in fact to all off mankind and yes even to those creations that we call our Brothers, namely those of the animal kingdom, then we will be fulfilling the plan that has been mapped out for us and by us, for remember that we are our own architects of our lives, and so we are responsible for all of our actions, and how they affect not only ourselves but others as well!!! Life can be glorious and yes is glorious when we live for each other by being unselfish in all our thoughts and ultimately our actions!!

That is what life is all about isn't it? It is, that when we accept that we are part of God and start to live as we know is pleasing to Him, then as life unfolds to us we can go along with its flow, knowing that as we do we are becoming ever nearer to that God head the one we call Our Father in Heaven!!

We bid you farewell and may you think upon what has been written this night and go forward with joy in your heart in the knowledge that you are part of God as He is part of you!!

Farewell dear friends, and little scribe. Farewell, and may the blessings of the One on High be with you now and always. Farewell.

May Allah be praised!!!

Chapter 5

November 19th 2003 12.30 a.m.

USE YOUR MIND INTELLIGENTLY

Once more we will begin our nights discourse with you and you no doubt wonder what it will be about?!! We have often talked to you about that illusive organ namely the mind. For it is responsible for all active thought, in fact it is responsible for All thought! Though not all thought results in action!! Man as yet is not fully aware of the great potential that the mind has! When he does then he will have matured! By which we mean he will have grown up! So to speak! For thought when properly understood and used intelligently is a wonderful tool, but it can also become a weapon of destruction by greed and the desire for power over others!! So you can see that Man has a lot to learn before he is allowed this knowledge of how he can use this tool called the Mind. At present he just uses his mind power in a very haphazard fashion, that is why the turmoil that your World is in at the present moment is mainly of Man's own making! And if you stop and think about it you will realize that, that, statement is the Truth!

Man's capacity for using his Mind or thought power for his own ends is very apparent. When you look at your big business tycoons and members of your so-called ruling classes!! For example your Political persons who very often start their careers with high ideals which soon become corrupted in the search for advancement and power!!! When Man uses his thought power for the benefit of his fellow man and by which we mean really for his benefit and not for his own personal gain, then you will see that your World can be a quite wonderful place to live in. But sadly we feel that that situation is a very long way off. If man and that includes woman, starts to train their offspring in the proper way, that is by being unselfish in all that they do, they will grow to adulthood with a clearer perspective of what life is meant to be! Being unselfish should be just the normal way of living and shouldn't even need thinking about, but No! they are brought up to believe that self comes first and other's last if at all!!! What a way to live!! You will never achieve a life of harmony all the time you seek to outdo each other, and for what? A bigger house? A larger car? Just symbols of greed if really looked at in the right light!! Man must learn to be content to live in harmony with his surroundings and not fight against them all the time. You do have enough, to live a good and pleasant life, do not store up for yourselves so called treasures of the earth that you will have to leave behind when it is your time to quit this earth plane and be as it were re-born once more upon the next one that is called by Man Spirit!!! And we can assure you that all your so called treasured possessions are of no use to you, when you are once again a Spirit person!!! You start off this new life of yours with Nothing, and we do mean Nothing! And the reason? You have no need for baubles and beads, you see life here for what it is and you see yourself for what you are or for what you have become!!! Have your earth lessons taught you anything? Here you will see the truth, and it is not always very flattering for the ego to see it stripped of its veneer!!! Once though you have overcome this first shock you will see that what was once thought of as necessary to your previous life style is not relevant over here!! There is no form of competitive behaviour, there is no need for it, though that does not mean that you do not have to lift a finger so to speak to help yourself! Your whole view on life will have altered, you will begin to see the value of what being unselfish can achieve, for on our realm unselfishness really is the normal way of living. You will think "why didn't I think upon those lines when I dwelt upon earth". Well perhaps you will if you feel that another incarnation upon that planet is necessary to your evolutionary advancement!!

Perhaps in the future those souls who will materialize upon earth will have a better understanding of their relationship with their fellow Man, then this globe of yours will be in a position to join those others from the distant space, where they have learnt the lessons of partnership and understanding long, long ago, and will be ready to welcome you earth people into the Brotherhood of Universal love! If you really work for this union, it will come about, but you have to start now, and that means thinking along the right lines. And that means living a God life, a good life in other words, its as simple as that!! I know you will say "Easier said than done"!! Well, you've been given a brain and a Mind to govern it, put the two together and use them as they were intended to be used, and not as is so often the case abused!! Those of you who are as we have said before this Thinkers of this world are also the teachers, and by example you can accomplish much, it may seem a small contribution to you, but all put together these contributions can be a force for good, and one that will last long, long after you yourselves have made the transition to our plane of existence! We will end our discourse on that note. Just remember that Thought when used properly is a wonderful tool, use yours and you will be amazed at the difference it will make to your lives!!

Chapter 6

November 20th 2003 1.45 a.m.

CHAOS IS ORDERED!

The subject for tonight's discourse is the life that awaits you on what is known generally as the World of the Spirit! When one mentions that word Spirit, it immediately conjures up in the minds of the listener of vague mysterious wraith like phantoms, that come and go almost like the wind, with no substance to them whatsoever! We can assure you dear friends we are nothing like that. We are, no, not flesh and blood, but we are solid and real, our bodies are observable and can be touched. We are to put it mildly just like you upon the earth. We are of course different in many respects, but we are nevertheless, human beings!! We are as we are, just as you are!! Though perhaps you upon the earth, when viewed by others who belong to places in outer space, could easily appear to them somewhat of the nature that could be called "Spirit"!! Vibration is what we are talking about. Each sphere or world or planet or whatever name you chose to call those orbs that you view in space, all vibrate at different rates. No two are alike!! And so the inhabitants of those spheres also are on different vibrationary wavelengths than you upon the earth, and yes even we who dwell upon the sphere known to you as Spirit! Vibration is responsible for all the so called difference of not only other worlds but also those who live upon them! There is Order in everything that can be seen and observed, even when to your eyes it may seem shall we say chaotic?!!! Nothing is left to chance, even your earth plane with its upheaval of your weather variations, are all following a pattern! What seems to you perhaps bewildering is the result of past atmospheric conditions, they form cycles that may last for hundred or thousands of your earth years, they are gradual in their expansion, and when you see the differences that are occurring they are actually the culmination of these years of silent life force in it's evolution! You are no different to other worlds and planets, yes and even ours, which will surprise you no doubt! For you tend to think that the "Spirit world" must be a world of order and tranquillity!! Well it is!! But it also lives and breathes just as your world does, but Ours has more stability in it's atmospheric conditions. There is no strident turmoil going on beneath the surface. Our vibrations are far more ordered, if that is the right word than yours!! Your dense planet rather attracts somewhat chaotic disturbances, because that is it's nature! In other words it is Natural for your world in it's present condition, and if you read that correctly, you may assume that in time it will alter and become more stabilized, in fact more like our world of existence!

Creation is a living force, it does not stand still! And as such there must always be change that is going on sometimes seen and at other times not until it is ready to break out, and then you begin to see this Creative force actually living and breathing and in the course of this activity, erupting and expanding and yes somewhat chaotic, which of course is very upsetting for those who have to experience its birth pangs!!! But it is inevitable and yes quite natural when observed from a distance and here we speak of time and not of space!!

All of this movement is part of your that is Mankind's lessons of life, you learn, you grow, you adapt! And these, shall we call them "lessons", are what you take with you when you depart your earth life and once more resume your life span upon our world, your earth one was just a necessary interruption of your growth upon the Spirit realm which is the real one, the one that goes on and on, even when it is upon other spheres of existence!! No, dear friends, you do not have to die each time you transfer to another dimension, your perception of where you are alters and so you are where you are expected to be! Do not try and fathom that out just yet, for you have to experience it for yourself, you cannot be told how it comes about, it just does, so accept that, as an explanation, even if it does not satisfy your curiosity!!

When you finally transfer your mind/spirit to the next plane of existence in other words your transition from your earthly vehicle, your whole vibrationary force will be heightened so that you are in unison with your surrounding's, then you will be able to adjust your "bodily" function and do things that at first appear to you as miraculous, but really are quite natural on this our and your plane of existence!!

As your "body" a loose term for you to understand, becomes accustomed to it's new surroundings you will experience all sorts of phenomena, that will astonish you, the freedom of your movement's and the thought power that governs them will give you great pleasure and as you gradually get used to this new found freedom of activity you will be shown how to use it for the benefit of not only yourself but for others as well. And by "others" we don't necessarily mean those upon the Spirit realm!! Food for thought dear friend. Your "world" of the mind is limitless and so are the action's that accompany it!! More "thought" for you to think upon!! This "new" life that you will inhabit or rather "re-inhabit"!! is one that is for you to explore your latent possibilities and put them to good use! Your life is one of active participation of all that is around and within you, you really do begin to Live as you have never done before. Look forward to this new dimension that you will one day inhabit, learn about what awaits you, leave behind your earth worn cares they have served their purpose in your character building, you are now ready for the new cycle of lives that you are to live on your upward/inward journey of the Spirit! A much misunderstood word that is used to denote the life to which we are all heir to.

We feel that we will end our nights talk to you little scribe and fellow travellers, for you have much to think about, and so we say to you Farewell and may the blessings of those upon high help you in your searching's for the truth. Farewell Brother!!

Chapter 7

November 25th 2003

THERE IS A NEW AGE COMING

There comes a time in most peoples lives when they stop, and stand still and think to themselves "Where am I going", and here they are thinking not of the body but of the inner being of light that they really are. We are now speaking of those who have allowed their eyes to be opened and sadly they are in the minority of the population, though we must say that there are amongst the younger population quite a number of deep thinking individuals who are earnestly searching for what they hope is the answer to their inner longing's for the Truth! There is an abundance of various teachings if you can really call them that!! That profess to be able to show a short cut to shall we say Salvation? They have dressed up age old so call mystery cults and pretend that they have answers for those of the New Age! They deceive only themselves if they did but know it! So much Mumbo Jumbo! What with their various incantations and weird postures, and incense that they think will increase their mental activity, when all it does is to make them even more confused than they were!!!

They imagine that "they" are the new priesthood to guide the students of occult philosophy, when all they do is plant in minds that are immature, ridiculous thoughts of visitors from Outer Space that will be able to inspire them in the esoteric way's of the deeper mysteries of the Universe!!! If there are to be teachers of those mysteries they certainly would not be the sort of worldly persons that are practicing these so called teachings!! A teacher who is capable of that vocation would be one of an Higher Order and one of Spiritual integrity, for they would know that if they are to instruct those who are the genuine seekers of the Truth, then it must be the Truth that is taught them! Though in actual fact it is merely awakening in those individuals what is latent in their minds, all they need is the right impetus, to bring forth the inner knowledge that they have previously learnt!!!!

Many of the young people will, shall we say, fall by the wayside and that must not be taken literally!! But that has always been the case right through the History of your earth planet!! For if it is looked at in the right manner you will find that illusion of one kind or another has always been prevalent on that dense little planet!! It is knowing what is illusion and what is not that is the prime lesson that has to be learnt by those who dwell upon that sphere!!! It is a case of learning that all is not what it may appear to be!! Once you have come to terms with that, then you can begin to shall we say start to unravel some of the hidden mysteries of this your own Universe!! Do not attempt to try and search beyond what is the perimeter of your knowledge of what you imagine is the, shall we say the edge of your known Universe, you cannot understand where your Universe ends!! For the edge as we have put it does not remain static, it is forever growing and yes even not always outwards if you can understand that statement!!! Remember that all life cycles and that includes not only worlds and planets and cosmic identities, have periods of rest and somewhat inactivity! A form of sleep if you like. But not what you call sleep. Inactivity does not quite mean what it says, for there is an inner life force to all life forms that does not slumber, words for you to try and understand, what is difficult for us to actually inform you, of this creative force that is all around and yes within all living breathing beings of creation! And that goes for the places upon which they dwell as well, remember that, when you are thinking about what is being written, and given to you, to try and understand! Creation and those who are created by which we mean you dear friends who are searching for the answer to the riddle of what is commonly called Life!! For the true life is not quite what you have been brought up to understand it as. There has always been this inner life that one lives that has always been somewhat of a mystery to the outer shell of the living person!! Most people do not even realize that they have an inner life which is another way of saying their inner perception of what is being observed by them day by day!!! We store up for ourselves these observations and one day we begin to sift through this inner knowledge that we have acquired through this life that we lead upon the plane of earth, and yes even beyond that plane if you get our meaning!!! Mysteries when understood cease to be mysteries and become liveable realities, all part of this thing called "life"!!! You have been given a lesson this night, think upon it, profit by it, and go forward and learn to Live the life that you have been put upon this earth of yours to live! And live to its full capacity!! Go on searching, you don't have to go to far off climes to find the hidden truths that you think you need, your journey starts and ends within yourself!! Think about that!! You are if you think about it, an aspect of the truth you seek! Do you understand what we say? You are truth and truth is you. To put it plainly, you are God made manifest. That is the Truth believe it and live it!!!

We end our nights discussion dear pupil and students and we leave you with the Blessings of Those on High!

Chapter 8

November 26th 2003 1.40 a.m.

LOVE ONE ANOTHER

Such a lot of mental activity is going on all over your little globe at the present time. No wonder so many of your youth are in a state of perpetual disorder! Their minds are being filled with such a lot of unhealthy thoughts, they are beginning to loose sight of what is right and what is wrong. Those two points are becoming blurred so that soon they will not be able to tell the difference!! This must NOT be allowed to take place! It seems that only a form of some catastrophe will bring them to their senses! And sad to say this also means those who are the parents of these young minds!! Your adults for far too long now have not shown their offspring what the real life is for, it has become shallow in the extreme. Moral behaviour has deteriorated out of all proportion and those little screens that seem to be in every home are one of the main courses of this lax behaviour. You are rapidly becoming a race of unhealthy thought patterns that are eating away at your moral fibre and if not stopped you will end up with no Spiritual thoughts at all!

Some of your more thinking older generations can see where all this is leading to, but they have not the stamina to alter what they see. They wring their hands and talk of times of the past, hoping somehow that by a miracle they will return! We say to you that is just wishful thinking, after two World wars and countless other conflicts still being perpetrated all over your globe, you have absolutely no hope of returning to those former days of peace and plenty!! You must start NOW to alter your thoughts and what is more, your actions which stem from those thoughts! As you can never go back to what was, you must see to it that what is happening now must be halted, it is not too late but it will mean concerted effort on the part of All Nations if this rot is to be stopped!!! And stopped it must be!! One of the main problems is this so called envy of what you in the Western world call Democratic life style! It is a camouflage for what we see as licentious behaviour. Self! Self! Self! That seems to be the normal behaviour these days and where is it getting you? Nowhere for you are going around in circles with no way out! Well there is!! But it will require discipline and will power of all peoples all over your world!! One country exploiting another! Is that the way you see as forward? No! it only breeds hatred and distrust and yes envy, for what those who have, by those who have NOT!! You must bring back some form of equality to the lives of those in the poorer countries, which in reality are sitting upon untold mineral wealth, that could make their lives one of joy and happiness, but they must not be exploited by those Nations with their advanced forms of Technology. What they have in that respect they Must learn to share it with those poorer nations and by share we mean share with no hidden strings attached to what they are sharing. For ultimately it is for the good of All, when all nations have enough of food and sustenance, then there will be no need to envy those Nations who it seems to us, flaunt their wealth in the faces of the poorer ones! No wonder there is so much turmoil going on in and around your World at present!! For you are affected by those thoughts that are sent out, for they attract others of equal stature and they then grow ever stronger. You must Stop and Stop Now!! Tomorrow will be too late! You do have enough of all the essential ingredients for a healthy and happy life style all over your planet, if only you learn to distribute it fairly and not for monetary gain all the time! Be fair and honest in your dealings and you will find that it will repay you a hundred fold, no more misery or poverty, they can become things of the past if you only start to trust each other, and when we say trust we mean that, that trust is one that will not be abused or exploited by the so called stronger nations!

Look not upon the colour of the skin or what is termed the religious background of any one country! There is room for all in this world of yours, and that means toleration of others beliefs. They may not be your beliefs but there is room for all shades of Religious understanding God sees beneath the surface, He is the God of all religious NOT just one, remember that. It is Man who insists on that assumption that His religion is the only one and all others must be obliterated! Do you really think that your God condones that action? If you do, then you have not yet understood what the word God stands for!! If you stop and think carefully then you would realize that God embraces All people regardless of what form their religious belief is. Religion as such means Nothing if it is not tolerant of others belief's!! Can't you see that? Whatever name you give to it, it is only a name and a name is just an expression, it is the deeds that are done that makes of Religion something to be proud of, and not just by those upon the earth and think about that!! Your deeds or actions do Not go unnoticed and one day you will have to account for them and that goes for Nations as well as for the individuals that make up those Nations!!!

Show those young souls that one day will take over from you, that loving one another with Universal love will bring about lasting peace and prosperity. That is the only way to live and lead a life that God intended us to live. Brothers in every sense of the word, for we are all the children of the One on High, be a family of Nations, one big family, and not these separate Nationalities that can't get on with each other. Learn to be tolerant in everything it really does work and is the only way forward if you want a life of stability and peace!!

We bid you farewell, dear friends upon the earth. This is your earth take care of it, not just for yourselves, but for those who will follow you. Farewell and may God bless you all!! Little scribe Farewell dear friend Farewell.

Chapter 9

November 28th 2003 Morning

Thoughts!

DON'T BELIEVE EVERYTHING YOU ARE TOLD!!

What are my thoughts? Well if I'm honest they are mainly about God and about the journey's we have to take to get "back" to "Him". Now that word "Him"! we all say that word if we are talking about God don't we? And yet can that possibly be the correct word to describe the "Almighty Being" that is the sole Creator of all that there is, visible and invisible!!! To my mind that Creative Essence of Life Force cannot possibly be categorised as a Being that we can identify as "Him". For that word signifies a "being" like ourselves doesn't it? We somehow feel comfortable with the word Him or God, or The Father as if we can nuzzle up to Him and be safe!!!

Now the lines upon which I think are these. There must be the Supreme Creator that as far as we are aware created All "things" or should I say all visible expressions of the Thought emanations that proceed form that unknown Life Force and Source! But the one that we, shall I say we as human beings identify with must be an aspect of that Prime creative source! And the word aspect" to my mind is no way near the explanation that we can give to the one we know as God! That is OUR GOD, for I do believe that there must be others of equal stature that other civilizations on other worlds or planets acknowledge as their God and they probably think of "Him" as the only one! Unless of course they are more advanced than us and can accept the concept of more than one "God creator", and here I am talking about the ones who are living "aspects" of the Supreme Unknowable Creative Source!!

I feel that that "ONE" understands the needs of "creations", that we are one of, who need a reference to identify with, one who they feel they can "talk" to either in thought, or prayer, or supplication!!! And so I think that all of these "God aspects" that are part of the "Supreme ONE" are in their own way the "Creators" of all that applies to US! Either we who are called "Human beings" or other's who we at present know nothing of!! Or perhaps some of us do!!!?

So what I am getting at is that Our God is the one who we know or rather try to know, "He" is our Creator and as such we are a part of "Him" as we have always understood we are! So all the "things" that we have been brought up to associate with God are correct up to a point!!! I feel that we in our poor way have no real idea of what the word God really means!! It is one of the many names that we humans like to label God as! How little we know! The Church and here I'm speaking broadly to encompass all religious teachings has not truly informed us, the "laity" the truth about the esoteric mysteries, perhaps it's because they don't really know about them and they may even not actually believe in them themselves!!! They "embroider" what little truth's they have been able to unravel, so as to make them obscure and sometimes unintelligent to ordinary people!! Some form of "power" is what they are guilty of, even if they do not see it in that light! If any of them were to read what I have written they would probably say it was Heretical and talk of either the Devil, or that I have a deranged mind!! Which quite frankly I have not! In fact I try to think I have an open mind on most subjects and am not persuaded by arguments just because they represent belief's of past ages!! We are meant to question and think for ourselves, its certainly not against the Law of God of which it seems to me we know very little of, because we have been deliberately kept in the dark and you know by whom!!!

When people really start to think and I do mean think about what this term God and Creation really means, and how they fit into this vast scheme of evolvement for all "living creations", then they surely must come to a conclusion that we have so much more to learn and try and understand about the complexity of what Life really is about and what it is for!!! We are so preoccupied with our own little "world" and I don't mean The World! That we don't stop and think about the true meaning of why we are where we are, and where we are ultimately going to and what it means not only to us but to God as well!!

I Love God and all he stands for, but I'm under no delusion that I will be fit to "see" him when I depart this life, How could I? How can we? If you really think about it? For God as God must be so, how can I put it? Perfect in every sense, that to actually be in his presence would be overwhelming, we would feel so utterly unworthy that we would want to hide ourselves from his very sight! But! We can "see" and appreciate all that He has created and that should be enough for us to know that we too are part of that creation and so we are part of God and knowing that, should satisfy us, "until" perhaps one day we may be worthy to sit in His Shadow!! Remember He is Our God and if there are others then we must honour them also. There is an Hierarchy of Creative Gods, that's what I believe, you may not, and that is your privilege. I'm quite happy with what I think, but I'm still open in my mind to any ongoing activities that will stimulate me into thinking and learning just a little more of what Life really is for and what I'm supposed to do about it!!! I think I'll end there for a while and perhaps resume this another time!!!

Well I've decided after reading the above that I have some more thoughts on the subject! You know that in the Bible I think it's in the Old Testament but I'm not sure! God says "Let us make man in our image"! Well that does imply that "he" had others around him of a like stature doesn't it? So even then there was "evidence" of more than one Creator wasn't there? I expect you'll say "they" were of the Angelic force, and not God as such! Well granted, but they must have been pretty "High Up" to be included in this Creative business mustn't they? That could account for the diversity of the creations that we can observe around us couldn't it? And who knows perhaps the Other Gods of other planets or Universes, "get together" now and again and exchange "ideas" and perhaps even certain "creative organisms" by which I mean creatures of the earth, the Sky and the Ocean's!! It could be endless!! Perhaps one day in the far off distant future it may be "Human beings" Mankind I'm thinking of who will transfer from one planet to another and even from one Universe to another in the evolutionary progress!!! I find that a wonderful proposition, and very, very exiting!! Just imagine what some of those other "Creations" might be capable of? What a lot of learning and understanding we will have to do. Perhaps some of these so called sci-fi things that people write about aren't so far fetched as they seem! Though I personally don't go along with all the warlike activities that they write about I suppose one could say that's just "artists licence" and leave it at that! And as for some of these extremely weird looking creatures half human it seems, well I don't think I buy that. Still who knows!! I did say I had an open mind didn't I?!!!

Thinking it over it seems to me that the word "Eternity" is a very apt one when you consider that this Universe and what it holds is probably one of many, that at present we know nothing about!! Would I wonder, does time as we are aware of it belong to all Universe's or does it alter, when we talk of "Light years" away when talking about other planets or galaxies it would seem that this Universe of ours is almost "endless", and yet I believe it does have how can I put it? A "perimeter"? an "edge" and what is it that lies beyond it? Is it another form of space? And does that contain other "Universe's" or what? Is "Space" so vast and endless that it can harbour numerous so called Universe's, some maybe small, while others could be like ours, or even perhaps gigantic, it almost seems without an "end" in sight!!! It is all so mind boggling that it beggars belief! We wonder about what it is that we see in "our space" and if we will ever be able to contact what we loosely call "alien life forms" I suppose we must include ourselves in that assumption for to other species that's how we must appear to them!! It is all so vast and to my mind incomprehensible to our immature way of speculating on "Creation" and how it all began! And we only think in terms of what we think we see, and there must be far more that vibrate at much Higher and faster velocity than our planet and so they would be quite invisible to our senses and yet they are realities to those who can observe then!!! We have such a lot of rethinking I fear regarding "Life out there"! and yes even life within our inner being!! We are such complex creatures and to my way of thinking rather immature ones at that!! Are we but prototypes or are we mutations of previous unknown species of what we term humanities?!!!

Such a lot for me to try and think about, I shall record all this and see if I can make any sense of it all, at least I can listen as it were to someone else talking and see if I agree or disagree with what it is that I have written about! So I think that this is really where I shall conclude my thoughts for today, wonder if on "listening" I shall start to think about other "things" that I would like answers to!!!?

Chapter 10

November 30th 2003 12.30 a.m.

YOUR CHARACTER!

We often think as we grow older about the life that we have lead, and where is it leading us to. Here we are speaking of you dear friends upon the Earth plane. Once you have reached our side of life, your previous one after awhile begins to fade in your memory, for there is so much more to the life that you will be leading in what is so often termed "The Spirit World" that, that, other life the one you have left behind you, almost seems like a "blurred dream", somehow it doesn't seem real anymore, and yet it was a reality while you lived it wasn't it? You did do all of those things that are still in your memory, you didn't imagine them, so what was the purpose of this life upon that lower plane? Sometimes you even wondered if it had any, when circumstances were thrust upon you, that perhaps resulted in unhappiness and disappointment! But now as you look back upon them you can see that there was a purpose there, even though at the time it wasn't visible! But all of these so called setbacks and perhaps disappointments were what has made you who you are Now! In other words they helped create the character that is the real you. I suppose we could say "warts and all"! For none of us are perfect, even if sometimes we may kid ourselves that perhaps we are!!! We all do at times, that's part of being human, but when we review our previous life cycle, prior to our taking up our new round of life's task's, we see what we were really like, and of course perfection didn't really figure high on the list of remembrance's did it? But then that is what that life was for! It gave you valuable lessons that you could not have experienced elsewhere! And now you are about to embark upon another round of lifetime experience's, though they will not be the same as your previous ones! But they may have a similarity on occasion, so your previous "lessons" will come in useful after all won't they? You see dear friends, life really does "go on" in spite of what some people may think! And of course say!!! But we know that those who really do think about what life is for know that is does continue nothing is wasted!!! You are still very much the you that you have always been, with the exception that now you are able to see who you really are and not who you thought you were, which is a very different picture that you have painted without knowing it!!! Life upon the Earth plane as you know is a training ground to prepare you for those future lives that you are to live and lead in your upward progress!

Do not feel dismayed at the thought of more lives! The one's to come are the glorious ones that you have earned, though perhaps you didn't know it when you were actually doing the learning! You will find that this new existence at first will seem quite familiar to you, and that is all for a purpose, it is to help you to adjust to this new and exciting life that opens up before you! You will "be" where it is that you have earned the right to be, we are all, shall we say "assessed" as to what is the best place for us to start off this new round of life experience's! Now here we are speaking of when your incarnations upon the earth have served their purpose in your evolutionary progress! We are not dealing here with those who are shall we say here for a period of rest and recuperation before returning once more to what is known in some cultures as the "Wheel of Life".

That subject has been dealt with before, as has the one that we are discussing now with you!!! There is nothing New that we can tell you, it is that we can give you a different perspective, a different slant as it were on a subject that awaits us all eventually, and that is the truth, believe that! The physical death is but a transition from one dimension of understanding to another, that opens up for you a vista of opportunities that you just cannot imagine existed! But here they can become realities as never before!! The world known to you as the "Spirit one" is far more alive and real than ever your earth one was, for here you see things as they are and not as upon earth as they appeared to be!! Quite, quite different, that is when you have got used to this new and vibrant dimension, where reality becomes a possibility and not just a wishful thought. By which we mean your new Life style, for you do live you really do, the opportunities that are opened up to you are based upon your own capabilities, which many of you have no idea that you even possess!! Life upon Earth taught you much, that sometimes has either been forgotten or pushed to the back of your mind as perhaps not being feasible while you tarried upon that lower sphere!

You will "expand here" your whole outlook will alter, because of the freedom of not only thought but also action that you now have, and believe us when we tell you that this freedom enables you to not only help yourself but others also, and those not always upon the world of the Spirit, if you get our meaning! You will have so much to learn and give that your "day's" and here we use that word in a hypothetical way, for "day" here is quite different to the one you were used to upon Earth!! Your "day's " then, will be full and will simply "fly past", so you see life really will be "fulfilling" in every way. The character that you have become because of your "earth life" will now serve you in very good stead. So look forward to this new round of life experience's with anticipation, you will not be disappointed believe us, for we do tell you the Truth for have we not been where you have been? And are we now where you one day will be? Life does go on it really does, and don't let anyone tell you differently!!! You have so much to look forward to dear friends. You are the fortunate ones for you have been given an insight as to what your life that awaits you is all about. Go forward with God's blessing and know that what you have been taught and learnt in your lifetime upon Earth has been worthwhile and there is and was a divine purpose to it believe that. We bid you all Farewell!! And to you little Brother scribe Farewell and know we are your Brothers, in truth we are! Farewell. Farewell!!

Chapter 11

December 6th 2003 1.10 a.m.

THE AURA

Welcome little Brother we are pleased that you are once more able to take up your pen and write what you are inspired to do.

How shall we begin? The Pathway back to our origins? Well that is a good start to any conversation is it not? And this pathway? What is it? And where is it? Is it a recognizable one? Or is on the inner plane of realization? We feel it is a mixture of the two, in actual fact it is the same, but with two different viewpoints! How can that be you wonder? Well if you think about it, it is very logical isn't it? You have a body that can be seen and you also have an inner one that is not observable and yet is in it's own way the most important one of the two!! For the outward one does the "living" so to speak and yet it has an impact upon that one that to the outward eye is not visible!! But it "sifts" through all the experiences that beset the outer physical vehicle, and in doing so it grows in stature, far outstripping that physical organ, it is this inner part that shall we say "survives" when the physical relinquishes it's life force, then it transfers to the other life called the Spirit!! For it is the inner force that is the Spirit that all along has been the guiding force for the outer vehicle. Or perhaps we should say it "should be" if we are living the right sort of life!! Sadly very few people even think about this inner being of consciousness, that dwells silently within! Yet each and every person upon your plane of Earth has this inner consciousness, it is called "The Christ Consciousness". Remember what the Master Jesus said to those disciples that were his friends when it was time for Him to leave them? And return to his Heavenly abode? "I go, but I leave with you the "Christ Spirit" that my and your Father has bequeathed to all of his children and that Spirit will always remain with you"!! What a wonderful gift He left with us, if only we can see and use it as it was intended to be used. It should be our guiding beacon of light that illumines our very being on its journey back through the darkness of our life upon Earth. When we live in the right way, that beacon of light illuminates not only ourselves but cast's it's radiance upon all who we come into contact with, on our journey along the pathway of Life!!

You know yourselves when you encounter one who has that light shinning from within, that embraces the outer shell called the physical body, you feel their inner spiritual presence, you actually do feel the better for having been in their presence, it may even have been just a stranger passing you by, but somehow their "Aura" has touched yours and you have literally benefited from it, even if you perhaps are not fully conscious of it at the time! That "Aura" the one that emanated from Jesus and touched all those who came within it's radius, which was one of immense strength that stretched far beyond the immediate locality of those around Him, that is what he left as his parting gift, so why don't we use it? Instead of hiding it inside our physical vehicle? Let it come out and be seen for what it is. That spark of the Divinity, that "Holy Spirit", that we are all heir to, when man releases this Spirit consciousness and lets it guide his life's actions then this world upon which you dwell will indeed be the Heaven to which you think is beyond this Earthly plane of habitation! Heaven is "everywhere" it is the perception of where you are at any given moment of time! Whether upon this Planet of yours, or where we, your Brothers in Christ Consciousness dwell! And yes even beyond our Plane of existence! Heaven is boundless and limitless, it starts within you and you take it with you as you journey ever upward to the Source of All Creation!

Look around you as you travel along life's Path, see in your fellow traveller's that Divine spark that we spoke of it is there if you look for it, in the lowliest and the Highest, it is in everything and everyone Open your eyes and we speak not of the orbs of vision that you think you see with!! The eye's we speak of are those of the inner consciousness, the ones you cannot observe and yet they are the true sight if you did but know it!

Sight is not always what you behold with the outward vision it comes from deep within your "phyci". That sight is never blurred for it "sees" what is beyond that façade of the physical body of reference, in other words it is aware of the true you, not the one you show to those around you, you are far more than that one, and deep down you know that what we say is the Truth! God has given you the opportunity to be like Him, yes, the opportunity, but you will have to learn how to use the gifts He has given you in abundance, and He gives the same to all equally, it is up to us how we use or abuse these gifts, He has given so freely and the greatest of these is that of the freedom of the will. See to it that it is used not only wisely but justly in all of your actions to your fellow man and to those creatures of the animal kingdom who are in truth our other brethren, who give love and ask nothing in return!

If Man can give Love and we speak of Universal Love to all living creations then your world will be a far better and happier place for you to dwell in, and when we say living creations, think about what that implies, it does not just mean creatures that roam the Earth it also means the very Earth upon which you and they live, and what it sustains, for you are custodians of this planet you do NOT own it, remember that!! Share and share alike! Give and do not count the cost, for Love is priceless and cannot be bought when it is given freely!!!

Your journey through life is one of learning and teaching and understanding, it is to fit you for the real one that you will one day inhabit, see to it that you have prepared yourself for this continuing journey of life or rather "lives", for there are many for you to live and learn and fit yourself, for the one that is called Eternal.

We leave you on that note make your journey one that you and your God can be proud of. Farewell dear friends upon this lower planet you call Earth. We are all Brothers indeed we are!!! And to the little person with the article that writes Farewell little one, peace be with you and God bless you. Farewell.

Chapter 12

August 22nd 2004

FINDING THE REAL ME!

Thoughts

When you reflect upon those years that have gone to make up your present life and you wonder just where have they gone to. For yesterday was many years ago and yet it seems now that it was but yesterday in your mind!! What if you were able to cast your mind back, not one, not two, not even three, but a matter of thousands, of years ago when first you trod this Earth plane!! Who were you? What were you? And now what are you? All of those various lifetimes one after the other, from Prince to Pauper, and maybe back to Prince again! Always learning just a little bit more, but no, not always learning, sometimes forgetting, and the next incarnation pulls you up with a start, and you wonder why in this particular life you are suffering, why? What have you done to deserve it? And there's no answer that you are aware of!! So how are we expected to improve ourselves if we don't know the cause that has landed us in the situation that we find ourselves in? Well I think I know the answer to that one, but it isn't much help to me I'm afraid!! The answer that I was going to give was. That our Spirit knows!! But is that any consolation I wonder!! We know that our Spirit remains the same regardless of who we are in any one incarnation, and of course it was or rather is our Spirit who chooses the incarnation that it thinks is best for our development. Or have I got that right? I don't think so, it must be for "its" the Spirit's development and we the human vehicle are a necessary component in its ongoing scheme or plan that will allow it to eventually leave this lower sphere for good and continue its true lifestyle upon the Spirit world where it truly belongs!

So exactly what is it that this earth existence teaches the spirit that is of use to it when it is free of its commitments upon Earth? I've always thought that we are the one's who need all of this learning, but going by what I've just written, we are necessary but only as a physical body for the Spirit to use and manipulate, because we, that it our bodily structure is made of dense matter suitable for this planet which Spirit is Not!! So if we were to be more in tune with our Spirit, or perhaps I should have said if the Spirit is more in tune with the physical body then things might be a lot easier for all concerned! I've always thought that the Spirit is the guiding force for our physical body, but perhaps it may find the physical vehicle that it chooses is not so co-operative as it should be!! And so that is what makes this life upon Earth for us human beings something of a form of battlefield, being pulled one way and that and not always understanding why!!!

So in a way its up to us to help the Spirit, by allowing it to influence us more in our every day living!! I expect in some cases its very glad to get rid of this encumbrance of a human body when it ceases to exist upon the Earth!! For when our physical body dies, that's it! For that body, and the Spirit can now take stock of what its physical vehicle has taught it during its sojourn upon Earth!! This is all the wrong way around as far as I am concerned regarding my thinking!! I thought the Spirit taught us and not we who does the teaching!!! I must really think about this, for its turning my previous assumptions upside down!!

We it would seem, that it the physical human being though quite important are not as important as we like to think we are. I know the Spirit is the one that lives forever and never dies and is the Real me and not this one that looks back at me from the looking glass!! So I that is this physical me must try harder to do what the Spirit me wants me to do, in fact I've got to be less selfish in always thinking of my bodily wants and think how best I can serve my Spirit so that it can once more live permanently upon the Spirit plane and not have to keep re-incarnating time and time again, and each time hoping that the physical person that is its "host" so to speak will this time around help it to be released from this wheel of Life that we think of is to do with our physical body but now I think it's the Spirit that has had to endure this trial and error existence on this Earth plane!!! And I truly feel very sorry for "it", which is really Me isn't it?

Well I never thought when I started this writing this afternoon that my previous thinking was going to be turned "topsy turvy". Wonder what I'll make of it all and also is there any truth in what I've written or am I on the wrong track so to speak! It's going to make me reassess all of my previous thinking. Though now that I think about it I've always thought and known that the Spirit is the Real One, its just that I never actually thought that it would be the physical me that was the instrument of Spirit's learning and that it relied upon me for this form of two way thinking if you can call it that!!! Think I'll finish on that note before it gets too complicated!!!

Continued!!!

But what is it that this physical body can give to the Spirit that is of real use to it on the Spirit plane? Is it the "character" that we become? That is important on the earth plane but is it relevant on the one of Spirit? Well yes! I think it is. For the Spirit when it is first manifested by the Soul is characterless isn't it? It's only by the physical body living day in day out year in year out that our character grows and becomes a very necessary part of us, so then that part of us must become part of the Spirit as it progresses through us!! So it takes on board as it were this character part of the physical body, as it matures because of its life upon earth!! Which if it hadn't acquired this human body it could not have known what "character is" even though to all intents and purposes it remains an invisible intangible part of a human being. So having a "character" must be a very important lesson for the human body to learn and "pass on" to its other self!! I wonder if acquiring a character has a lot to do with being in tune with our Higher self our Spirit, for character is formed I think by being unselfish in every thing you do and think, and that must I feel be because the Spirit has influenced the physical. So it is a two way form of tuition isn't it?! We have so much to be grateful for to our Spirit for having chosen us in the first place to be it's other half in this present incarnation!! So we must try not to let it down, and listen to it when it is trying to influence us to do the right thing and not the wrong thing, which often looks the more inviting if a decision has to be made!!

After all this writing I feel I know my Spirit just a little bit better than when I started this writing! I hope so and I feel closer to the real me than I have done before. So this has all been worthwhile as far as I am concerned, and I must strive to make it last, for its for both our benefit's isn't it? I feel somehow that I was meant to put pen to paper this afternoon. I'm really looking forward to one day not just meeting my Spirit but becoming him once more. I hope then that I can see if the me that was the physical one has done my job of learning well, and that the Spirit me can be proud of its choice or earthly companion!

Now this is really where I finish! With my thinking and hope I've learnt something worthwhile!! Time will tell I'm told!!!!

Chapter 13

August 23rd 2004

MORE ABOUT ME!

Thoughts

After my thoughts of yesterday regarding the Spirit and its bodily counterpart which is me for that's who I am writing about! I've had, or rather am having more thoughts about the two "roles" that are played out by those two parties! First I think I'll try and deal with "my Spirit". Though as I'm not actually in "physical" contact with "him" even though "he" can and does influence me! So he must be able to be in contact with me on a personal basis!! Well now what I'm going to write is purely theoretical on my part and is coming from my mind, which of course is governed, as it were by my Spirit, so I suppose in actual fact what is written does emanate from him and yet there must be times when the thoughts that I get are from "me" this physical me, sort of independently, perhaps when the Spirit me is doing its own thing!!! Not sure I quite understand all of that, still I did say it was theoretical or hypothetical didn't I?

Well now regarding the Spirit's part in all of this! This spirit, the one that "looks after me", I feel is one of many, perhaps six or even seven of "me" that exist in Spirit form upon other spheres of the Spirit World!! But as I don't really know anything about "them" I can only deal with the one who is personal to me while I am a physical being in this particular incarnation!!! Well this one

I feel is the one that has been the "mainstay" of all the various incarnations culminating in this present one!! And during these various incarnations "it" the Spirit has had to accept the learning's and experiences of those various bodies that it was responsible for, how can I put it? Responsible for bringing them into "life" as it were!! For it was the Spirit who in between the incarnations of physical bodies, who had to choose what it considered was the right one for it to "inhabit" during the next incarnation!!! Now just supposing that, well it didn't make a mistake but the one it chose didn't "turn out" quite how he had planned and thought it would!! The physical body may have been a wayward type of being, not easily influenced by the Spirit that was its mentor and guide!!!

So then there might well have been some sort of "tug of war" between them, ending only with the demise of the physical body and the release once more of the Spirit!! Who probably deserved a rest from all of this trauma, and probably thought "I'll be more careful next time"!!! So looking at it in that light, it's the Spirit who does the incarnating and the physical vehicle is just the means with which to do it!! So much for the physical and its feelings of importance! Which I think are misplaced!

So then this last or perhaps first spirit has a great responsibility hasn't it, in learning through its surrogate body, what it has come down to this lower plane to try and understand the "Why" of why it had to find out who it really is and what part it is expected to play in the scheme of "things". Meaning, what "being created" is all about and what it is for!!! And all that it is learning through these various bodies upon the physical plane, will have to be eventually assimilated by those other "spirit essences" that I mentioned in the beginning, so all of this trial and error on its part is a great responsibility for it to shoulder I feel, for the actual evolution of the "Soul Essence" all depends upon the outcome of its learning. I'm almost tempted to say "Poor Spirit" but that's like commiserating with oneself isn't it?!!!

I'm beginning to understand just what the Spirit (Me!) has to go through during all these Earthly incarnations that has kept it away from its real home "The World of the Spirit". I should imagine that sometimes it wishes that Soul had found an easier way of learning all about itself, one less arduous and less hazardous in the journeying that it has had to take!!

When I think about all of those other "me" (that I know nothing about) that have been the cause of Spirit having to live for so long just longing to get back to where it came from in the first place, I feel rather guilty. Though I do know that the Spirit does have some respite from its duties regarding the physical body, so perhaps it isn't all work and no play after all!!!

Now to investigate the role of the physical human being in this ongoing saga of life or lives!! And it won't take long I fear, because I'm only aware of this life that I'm living. I know there have been many more, I was told of two of them, and I wasn't too keen on what I learnt about them! But now I know that really they weren't anything to do with me, each incarnated being is quite separate, and though there may be similarities that's all they are, just similarities and nothing more. Whatever remembrances are recorded are to do with the physical vehicle that was used at the time, it was the Spirit that had to cope with them and sometimes try and make amends for what the physical side of it had done that was wrong, because it had not listened to its Higher self, and so it was the Spirit and not the physical that had to shoulder the blame and try with the next incarnated human being to make recompense in some way, and that could account for some people feeling they have a very hard life and wonder why and feeling they didn't deserve it! Which of course they don't, because what was done to warrant this was done by another being and not by them. But it's the Spirit that is doing the real suffering, because of its responsibility regarding that previous one who transgressed!!

Justice is done, though we don't always see it in that light, we don't, but our Spirit does!! And it accepts the verdict without question!! After all this, I have a great deal more respect and love for my Spirit and I pray that I can be the one who will be the means to release "it" Me!, from the bondage of these incarnation's!!

I think that this is where I will bring this to a close. I feel I have learnt something today, something that I was unaware of when I got up this morning.

And to my Spirit. I give you all my love, and thank you for this life that you have given me to explore. Thank you and God bless you and me!!

Chapter 14

August 25th 2004

KARMA!

Thoughts

Karma! Cause and Effect! So what is done in a previous life catches up with you in this one!! But wait!! We are assuming that "we of today" were the ones of yesterday!! But physically we just cannot be! For once this mortal body has served its term upon earth and then departs it, well that's the last you see or have anything to do with it! And the You is your Spirit!! So looking at that in a logical way it is the Spirit and the Spirit only who was around in that previous incarnation and is still here in this one!! Do you see what I am getting at? It can't be the physical body in this incarnation that is responsible for what happened in the previous one, so who is?! Yes! The Spirit you, that one that goes from one incarnation to the next! And chooses the appropriate vehicle that it considers the right one for it to make recompense, if that is required, because of the previous life style that has resulted in this "Karmic tie"! So even if the physical being on the previous incarnation was responsible for certain "acts" that perhaps result in bad Karma, it is the responsibility, nay the duty of the Spirit to see that the one that it "inhabits" in this incarnation is the instrument that will carry out what those Karmic ties decree!!!

It may seem somewhat unfair on the physical vehicle in the

present incarnation to have to be the one to make amends, but this vehicle is the "host" for the Spirit to dwell within when it wishes to, and so the Spirit will see to it that its "host" does not have to suffer unduly for those past indiscretions of its previous "host" or vehicle of its previous incarnation! In actual fact there is a form of justice in all of this, because the physical vehicle of today may well incur Karma of its own, good or bad! And it will be its successor who will have to clear the debt!!! Now you will say "Well if we have a Spirit that looks after us, why doesn't it stop us from incurring Karma"!! Well there is an answer and I think you know it! Its called "Free Will" and even the Spirit is not allowed to tamper with that! Also our Spirit is not always with us all of the time. And so the physical body can and does do what it wishes! Right or Wrong!!! So you see we really should try and live in harmony with our Spirit for the benefit of all concerned!! And the sooner we do this then any Karmic ties would be for good and not bad and that would mean that our successor would have an easier life style, so you see what affects one does affect others as well, even if on the whole we are unaware of it!! As we progress upon the path of evolvement we begin to understand the laws that govern our Universe and our life and so we should work within them if we wish for a life of stability. Its knowing what to expect and incidentally what is expected of us!!! And that means what our Spirit expects of us, for though we can live our own life, it does reflect upon our Spirit self in no uncertain terms!! The whole reason for Spirit having to undertake this long and arduous journey of "self discovery" and sometimes the one it chooses to incarnate in, is not always as compatible as it probably thought it was going to be when it planned its next incarnation in the human body of its choice!!!

Though it tries to take everything into consideration, there are elements that are beyond its control!! For example the "genes" of both physical parents that are to be the vehicle of procreation of the new child!! These cannot be interfered with, that is something that the Spirit has to contend with as the child matures into an adult! So you see its not always that straight forward for the Spirit is it? Also there are other influences, outside ones, that the Spirit was unaware of, it just cannot plan for every occurrence that may influence the vehicle of its choice!!! That is what life is all about and what it is for!!! That is what creates the character that the Spirit needs, and it gets it via the earthly body, its partner, its companion, upon this particular part of its evolutionary progress that will eventually take it back to its Soul Creator! Once these earth incarnations have ceased, then Spirit will no longer need a host body within which to dwell. For it can at last "Be Itself" and from here on it is responsible for its own actions, and its life, though perhaps not all plain sailing will be more rapid in its form of Spiritual evolution! For Spirit will be with its contemporaries its friends not only of the past but from the present as well. For it has returned time and time again to the World of the Spirit and not only during but also between incarnations, where its stay is longer. The Spirit has friends, teachers, and guides that have been, shall we say, educating it, so it will be a joyful reunion knowing that this time it is going to be permanent!! You wonder how it will look, that is it "spiritual physical" appearance!! It all depends upon the individual. Sometimes a "physical" appearance can be an advantage especially when renewing ties with loved ones from today's incarnation. Gradually though the appearance alters as we all do and as their's has also done, but this is only temporary, that is the human appearance for we all have to progress and still being tied as it were to the physical memories does not help in that progression! We all learn, for that is Life isn't it?

You wonder do we still create Karma on the Spirit World? And the answer is, Yes we do! But not to the same extent as was done upon Earth! Here, we learn how to adapt, and if for instance we do not at first "like" someone, we look within ourselves and find out why we feel like that and that way we can rectify that straight away, it does not build up!! We don't have to love the other person, but we learn to compromise and toleration is the answer!! And who knows it could result in a lasting and life long friendship!! So when the Spirit is completely liberated from its earthly commitments, it can then start to live the life that for so long has been denied it, one more step along the path of progress.

I think that the above brings us up to date regarding Karma and the consequences that arise from it. Of course there's lots more and we have only skimmed the surface so to speak, for Karma is far deeper than what that word seems to imply! For not all Spirits feel that it is their responsibility to rectify past wrong deeds. Of course it is, and that is something that spirit must come to terms with if it wishes to progress!!! Life as we have said is not always straightforward, and being a Spirit does not make of you a Saint!! There are still lessons to learn and we hope profit by!!

We bid you Farewell travellers upon the Earth plane, and to you dear Brother, this discourse started out as yours but has ended as ours!! Farewell little friend Farewell.

Chapter 15

August 26th 2004

THE FUTURE BEYOND THE FUTURE!!

More Thoughts!!

What exactly is the relationship that exists between Body and Spirit? We tend to think that somehow our spirit must resemble the physical body in some way. But why should that be the case? After all the Spirit as far as we know is "ageless" in terms of what we think of as age! It has existed and lived here upon Earth as well as in the World of the Spirit for maybe hundreds if not thousands of what we term earth years!! And it incarnates in a human body when an incarnation of a human is needed, by the Spirit to further its development! And the human that will be its physical dwelling place only survives because of the Spirit that inhabits its body! And with each incarnation the Spirit chooses another human embryo to be its companion for the human's life span. But that doesn't mean that each incarnated human being that the Spirit "takes on" so to speak need have any resemblance to the previous one!! In fact in some cases the Spirit may choose to be incarnated in the body of the opposite sex if certain lessons are to be learnt that requires this change of venue!!!

So really this physical body will last only as long as the Spirit desires it to, and then that body is no more!! So really any memories of past lives lived are relevant only to the Spirit and not to the present physical body that the Spirit is inhabiting in this incarnation!! So when someone say's they remember part of a past incarnation it was not of them personally but their Spirit and that memory is part of the spirits previous life and has nothing to do with the present person who is host to the spirit in this incarnation!! I think that so often we mistake that memory that is form the minds store of memories as one of "our own" that is the physical bodies memory bank that it acquires during its life time!! The only memories that apply to that body are of this lifetime and not of another lifetime that was not theirs!! It may sound confusing but its logic really, when you think about it, and accept that it is only our Spirit who has this ability of not dying as we of the physical will one day have to!! Sobering thought is it not!!

So really we ought to know more of this Spirit that dwells in the house that we call our body!!!

Do we I wonder think of our Spirit as a "replica of ourselves"? Perhaps when our "transition" takes place and we, that is our Spirit returns to the realm of the Spirit it will be met and associate with loved ones and others who remember you as you were as a physical identity, and so the Spirit assumes this physical looking identity until such times as it feels it is no longer of any relevance to its present mode of life here in the Spirit World, where it will remain until either it needs to re-incarnate once more upon the Earth plane, or alternatively it may not need to and so it can be "itself" again!!! And what self is that I wonder?!! For Spirit is able by thought to create for itself whatever identity it feels is appropriate for a particular period of its ongoing life. We are told that the Spirit is "Spirit essence", but to us upon Earth that statement is somewhat bewildering, for we do not know what exactly "Spirit Essence" is!!! Do we?

We know that we are made up of various substances that make our body "solid matter" so to speak! But "Spirit Essence", well we have no yardstick with which to judge it by have we? It's of a "substance" for want of a better word, that can materialize as a solid and warm human being and then disappear leaving no trace whatsoever!! We can't do that with our body can we? All rather bewildering to our senses, which demand some kind of "proof" that is rational and logical!

But perhaps those two words have no real meaning on the Spirit world, for their laws and limitations cannot be understood by us upon this lower sphere of dense matter!!!

We do have much to learn not only about our Spirit counterpart but about ourselves also!! I'm sure that for one thing, our Brain has a greater capacity for all sorts of things that the Mind could call upon it to do, but at present we are not in a physical condition to be able to take advantage of what might be shown us that we are capable of doing!! Perhaps one day in the distant future when we are more in tune with our Spirit Self we shall be shown just what we are capable of when we put our Mind to it!! And it is this mind that is the key that will unlock all the treasures that lie in wait for us to tap into!!

We must I feel get to know more about our Spirit side of our nature, become in tune with the universal laws of cause and effect, Search more for the treasures of the Spirit and leave the so called treasures of the body that we spend a lifetime acquiring, where they can rot and disintegrate, for they are of no use to us when we leave this body behind and resume once more our Spirit body of Light and even that expression needs to be understood doesn't it?

So much to learn and unlearn no wonder we need so many visits to the Earth plane in our search for the meaning of life and what is true and what is false!! And of course I'm speaking of the Spirit and not this little bundle of ego's that we call a physical body that doesn't seem to last for very long does it? But still we now know that its our Spirit that is the really important one and as it has Eternity on its side, we needn't worry too much need we?

Just live day by day and let the future take care of itself, because our future is the NOW at least for the physical vehicle it is, and the Spirit? Well it knows what its future holds for it, for with each successive incarnation it is nearer to what it set our to achieve, Union once more with its Creator, and perhaps the start of yet another journey of discovery upon a distant sphere, but not upon the planet Earth!!! That journey has been completed and need never be repeated!!

Chapter 16

August 29th 2004 2.30 a.m.

GET TO KNOW YOUR SPIRIT!

Welcome once again dear Brother. We say unto you, know thyself!! Just words but the meaning is very clear. Not many people can say "yes, I do know myself". For to know oneself can take many many lifetimes, and still one doesn't know oneself completely! And really is that any wonder? For we are very complex creatures, with many sides to what we term ourselves! And is there a reason for this you wonder and the answer "is yes there is!" For this physical being that we think of as ourself is merely a disguise that we put on to show to the world, but the Real person dwells deep within this covering of mortal flesh and that "real one" is the one we know as Spirit!! We say "we know as Spirit" but that one is far more difficult to find, because we never (that is the physical body) we never really allow that one to be recognized as our true self!! Yet both "bodies" are a necessary part of each other!! The physical takes us all our time just keeping it in an active condition and so we do not really pay attention to that side of us, that though hidden from physical sight is the main reason for the physical being upon the Earth in the first place!! For to the Spirit this Earth is an alien environment to which is has to be part of in its upward journey of evolution!!

This Earth has been termed a "training ground" and to most people that means the physical bodies training ground. But principally it is for the benefit of the Spirit, yet the Spirit relies upon the physical part of its make up to gain the knowledge that only "it" is capable of attaining upon this lower sphere of dense matter! You wonder why this has to be, for if we are principally Spirit what can this Earth experience teach it that is relevant upon the plane of Spirit where ultimately we all have to go to once we have completed this part of life's cycle!!

Each day presents to the physical body a series of shall we call them "challenges". Not seen as such by the body who is witnessing them, but challenges they are!! It is how we meet and overcome them, that is the important thing, it is what is known as building your character, you spend a lifetime doing just that, but it is a necessary part that the Spirit can take with it on "it's" continual journey in it's search for it's true identity!! Yet we leave behind this physical body don't we, when it's time for the Spirit to depart from it!! It maybe forgotten but it's impact upon the Spirit is lasting!! With each incarnation the Spirit learns more about itself, for it does do the incarnating through that body of the physical, that though just a temporary residence is the only way it can acquire what it needs, "a character"!! One that will sustain it through its journey back to it's soul essence and onwards and forever upwards!

Now you will ask, what has the Earth's experiences to do with the Spirit if it's main home is the Spirit world and surely those self same experiences do not occur there as well do they? Well yes they do, but not exactly the same in the sense of being identical to those upon Earth. But those experiences have taught Spirit how to adapt to similar circumstances that may occur, for life upon the Spirit plane is not, shall we say, "All a bed of Roses!!" Now that will make you sit up and wonder what we mean by that!! Well it's just "Life" for life upon the realm of the Spirit goes on just as it does upon the Earth plane. You don't always know what is "round the corner". And let us face it, you would not want everything planned out for you to the last detail would you? You are an independent being of high intelligence and not "knowing" keeps you active mentally as well as "physically" and we speak here of the Spirit which to us who are Spirit we think of as just as physical as we have always been!!! Different yes! But mentally very much the same. For as you are aware the "Mind" is the driving force behind everything we do and always have done!! Only here upon the Spirit plane it is far more active in every way! For here you can see immediately the results of your thought actions, you see how they affect those around you, you don't have to wait like you did upon Earth to see the results of them. And so you learn how to "think" before you act. And that does not mean that you are perpetually having to regulate your thought mechanism!! It becomes automatic through use!! We won't say another lesson that you have learnt, but in actual fact it is!!! It is all those so called "lessons" that are character building, but we don't see it like that do we? So you see, what we learnt upon Earth does have it's place upon the Spirit realm doesn't it? It's such a pity that when earthbound we aren't more aware of the spirit side of our nature, for if we were life would be far more harmonious in every way! It will come about one day and perhaps sooner than you may think!! For the youth of today, that is those who think deeply, and there are more of them than you realize, those youth's are turning to the Spirit for actual guidance, though they would most likely be the last to admit it shall we say openly, but never the less, they are seeing life in a different way to those of the older generations who are perhaps set in their ways!! They the youth can see the futility in many of the things that have been sacrosanct for so long but are no longer relevant in today's society! The older generation do not like what they see at present, but this moral laxity will pass and they the youth will come out of it stronger both physically mentally and spiritually, once they have understood that freedom of thought and action carries with it responsibility towards those around them and yes to those also beyond them!!! The world is shrinking in more ways than one and out of all of this visible chaos will come stability and peace and that will come about through the release of "Universal Love" which will be the guiding force for lasting peace and understanding!!!

In other words the Spirit side of Man's nature will no longer be hidden, it will be seen as it is and was meant to be seen as the guide to right living. Spirit and Body, Body and Spirit two sides to the "One coin" Heaven on Earth, it can be, you know, all it needs is the will to make it so, and that will come from Man's Spirit when he lets it come to the fore in every thing he does!! And yes thinks!! For it is through Thought that that action takes place and when that thought is from the Spirit and acted upon in a spiritual manner than you will see what a wonderful world this can be and was always meant to be by the Creative Force that brought it into being!!

Farewell friends of the Earth.

We bid you goodnight and Farewell little Brother of this nighttimes discourse, peace be with you dear friend, peace be with you!

Chapter 17

August 31st 2004

THE BRAIN!

Just Random Thoughts.

What do we really know about the Brain? This Brain is like a family of "computers" that get activated by electrical currents sent out from the Mind in a form of "Picture Thoughts" made up of thousands if not millions of little "dots" that vibrate and are alive. Now we don't as yet use all of these "computers" we will in time, I think when we have progressed Spiritually and know how to handle the powerful tool that is the Brain that is governed by the Mind that is then controlled by our "Spirit"!!! The thought's that emanate from the Mind at present do not do it justice, but then we at present are rather infantile in most of what we think aren't we?

These pictures that are sent along the lines of communication to the Brain are all full of electricity and that is what triggers the Brain into positive creative action! Quite a lot of these pictures are stored in the appropriate sections of the Brain and are shall we say automatic in their functions! In other words we don't have to think about what it is we want to do. The Brain does that for us!! But when it comes to original creative thought, then the Brain has to be shall I say "Wide Awake" to the incoming thought waves and has to make rapid decisions for what is being required by the Mind substance that is under the control of the Spirit!! Though I don't think the Spirit is always doing the controlling so to speak!! I think sometimes it just "observes" what the body is doing "on it's own" in a way allowing the Mind a certain amount of "freedom of Thought"!! That way the physical body is learning and progressing and ultimately passing on it's gained knowledge to the Spirit!! I suppose some people would call it making "Karma". All cause and effect!! Though the Spirit does have the final say regarding that!!

So our Brain has a lot to do especially when it gets two or three conflicting signals and has to decide which one is the most important and takes first place and the others can "wait their turn"!! Which sometimes means we've forgotten them, until the brain gets jolted into activity and remembers them!! All of this "activity" is activated by electricity which we seem to be made up of in a peculiar way, that is why we can be influenced by outside forces especially when certain people invade our force field without our permission so to speak!! That is why we should always make sure that our "protective shield" is in place if we are to come into contact with relative strangers who we know nothing about!!

Psychic phenomena and other forms of electrical discharge, for example lightning can be quite disruptive to a sensitive person's Aura and can cause a form of upset to their equilibrium which has to be re-adjusted before they can resume normal activities!! As you know everything, either animate or inanimate has its own force field both in and without of its "body" so to speak. Learn how to use this force field to your own advantage, in other words, don't let "it" influence you if you do not wish it!!!

So now back to the Brain and its various functions, though sadly we only use a fraction of what is available to us, in time no doubt we will be able to but the time is not right, yet!! But when it is, then we will really be "super human beings". These things take time if they are to be used in the correct manner and at present Man cannot even control his own emotions, so it would be chaotic if he were to be given this knowledge before he is able to control himself let alone the Brain that is a tool so powerful as to be almost unbelievable!

When he has become Master of this hidden force and when he knows how to use it wisely, then and only then will he be welcomed into the Universal Brotherhood of other Planets, and even then he will be but a novice when compared to these other advanced nations upon those far off spheres!

Your World, though at present is in a very unstable condition in time it will "right itself" for it has been programmed to do so. It has been deemed a very useful sphere for the training of the human organ known as "Man" and that word incorporates his opposite for the Female of the Species is to become a "force for stability" in her own right. Man and Woman are complimentary to each other neither being the superior over the other, as seems to be the case at present. This has to alter and soon if you wish for a world of peace, for it will be the Women of the World who will bring this about, in spite of Man's opposition to it!!! Man and Woman are one if they only knew it, and are not as separate as they may think!! One day it may come about that the "genders" will merge as it were, separate but never the less "together" they will be able to become "one or the other" if they consider it advantageous to those concerned!! We cannot go any further in that direction for much has to be thought about before that change can come about. And it would involve considerable change we are told. But it is a possibility in the future!

We feel that this is where we will depart from this discourse that was not ours to begin with, but we know the little scribe understands!

And so we will bid you all Farewell.

And thank you Brother for your courtesy in letting us take over!!

Farewell dear friend for you are a dear friend believe that.

Chapter 18

September 3rd 2004 2.45 a.m.

THE BOND BETWEEN THE SPIRIT AND THE PHYSICAL

The Spirit! We talk about our Spirit as if it's a separate entity, quite apart from our physical body are we correct in that assumption? Well in a way yes and no!! For though our Spirit is the guiding force in our life upon the Earth "it", the Spirit is not always present, shall we say, within the physical body, it comes and it goes! But when it is absent from the body it leaves behind an aspect of itself which is what we know as our "conscience"!! So the physical vehicle is never really alone! And yet it does not always heed what that conscience tries to tell us! And so when our spirit takes control once more there is quite a lot of "catching up" to be done!!

When our Spirit originally decided upon this incarnation and chose it's vessel that was to be it's companion during that earthly incarnation it chose in a way an unknown quantity, it had a pretty good idea of the body that it was going to use but it had to let that physical body have freedom of choice. And that is what we call "Free Will". Our Spirit is here to learn certain lessons that will be of use to it when it returns to the Spirit plane either for good, or as a temporary visitor between its various incarnations. But to get the full benefit of this learning it has to allow the physical body to shall we say "Live it's own life", make it's own decisions, and yes make it's own mistakes, which is all part of this so called learning about life!! Now if the Spirit was constantly on hand the physical body would in a way be inhibited in it's own actions, and the lessons that the Spirit wanted to learn would in a way be curtailed, for Spirit would want to influence the body, which would quite often not only stop mistakes being made but would also negate any lessons that should have been learnt!! So Spirit has to stand back and sometimes just let the physical "get on with it" and make a mistake!! For making mistakes is the only way that some of us are able to learn a lesson that will allow the Spirit to progress. It may seem like a paradox for the Spirit to allow this to happen just so that it can profit by the mistake of the physical, but that is what Life is all about isn't it? We overcome and then we are stronger when that situation comes our way again, and that goes for our Spirit as well!! Our physical body is the one that the Spirit chose in the first place and it has to accept that it doesn't always do what is expected of it!!! For as we grow from youth to maturity and beyond we are acquiring knowledge, which then in turn is passed on to our Spirit.

So our Spirit shall we say is kept on "it's toes", not quite knowing how its companion body is going to react to circumstances, so in a way it's a bit of a tussle, a sort of tug of war, but a very necessary one if the Spirit is to learn what it needs to in it's present incarnation upon Earth through it's chosen vehicle the physical body!!! This really is a chance for the physical to show what it is made of, and because the Spirit allows it this freedom of choice, it sometimes is very surprised at the way the physical body has independently become a person in it's own right. And incidentally the Spirit can be very proud that it's chosen "friend" has turned out so well. For the bond between Spirit and body grows very strong, and sometimes the Spirit is very reluctant to "let go" of its life long companion!! For once that time comes for it's transition back to the Spirit realm, it has to say farewell to that body that has meant so much to it in its sojourn upon Earth. So you see this physical vehicle is so very important to the Spirit's evolution, and it leaves an indelible imprint upon the Spirit's, shall we say "Psychic"!!? In choosing the body that it is to become attached to during the life time of that body is a very important decision that the Spirit has to make before that physical body is brought into existence! And if by any chance the Spirit makes a wrong decision then that particular incarnation can become a very tricky one for it and can result in perhaps bad Karma being made that it will have to rectify during another incarnation!! So it's choice has to be very carefully thought out! But it cannot always foresee how it's physical companion will react once it has reached maturity, for remember the body has it's own idea's as to how it wants it's life to progress and the Spirit's needs are not always taken into consideration especially if the physical body is wilful and has shall we say "a mind of its own", figuratively speaking!!

Life can be quite a battleground, but if the Spirit is wise it can always find a solution that goes in it's favour!! All part of the learning curve, you could say!! For after all, even upon the realm of the Spirit, not everything is as "straight forward" as people may think it is going to be!! But then you wouldn't want everything to be "cut and dried" would you? The Spirit needs an impetus for living, just as you the physical does while dwelling upon the Earth!! Nothing really changes, and yet it does, when you stop and look at it and take stock of what life has taught you and here we are referring to your Spirit you, for after all that's the main one in that partnership of Spirit and physical upon earths short journey isn't it? The one that leads to the eternal one that we all take on our way back "home"!!!

So that choice that the Spirit made that resulted in you the physical being the person you are, well you have the Spirit to thank for giving you the physical, the opportunity of a life upon Earth, so live it as best as you can and know that you are an important part of your Spirits own life that continues when yours leaves off, don't be sad at that remark for the real you lives forever and you have been a part of that life and one that will never be forgotten by that unseen you!!

We leave you there, remember you are important. And you are necessary in the scheme of things!

Farewell friends upon the earth.

And to you little Brother be patient just a little while longer and you know what we mean. Farewell and we extend our Love to you as well!

Chapter 19

September 4th 2004

WHAT DO WE KNOW THAT WE DON'T KNOW?!

Thinking about the transition that we make from one dimension, the earth, to the next dimension, the Spirit. Now we know that the word transition is another word that people seem to prefer to the word Death! But whatever name you call it, it all amounts to the same thing! Our physical shell of a body remains while our true self the Spirit makes this other journey to the next dimension! Now we know that the Spirit that is our real self was the one that chose the physical body to be it's dwelling place upon earth, so that implies that our Spirit "body" was already upon the Spirit plane and may well have been there for a considerable period of what we know as earth years!

So going a step further along this trail of the Spirit, as a being that was already familiar with the Spirit world, in fact you could call it its "homeland" it should also be aware of all of the procedures that we are told the newly arrived spirit has to go through! So it would come as no surprise to it, for it's repeated this procedure many, many, times before, and no doubt in some case's will continue to do so. Depending upon which lessons it feels it needs to elaborate on!

Well! In between earthly re-incarnation, what is it's life like upon the Spirit plane? Are there certain "areas" so to speak, that those Spirits who are only there on a "temporary" basis go to even if it amounts to many, many years of our time! Now what is their "day to day" living, what sort of life do they live? It seems that when people and that's usually those who believe in spiritualism talk about "the Spirit World" it usually ends just there! They do not delve very deeply, lot's of questions remain unanswered as far as I can see!! And yet to the person who is a genuine searcher after the truth they need to know the facts and do not wish to be put off with the words "Oh the Spirit people are very happy, no more aches and pains its wonderful where they are" all very nice to hear that, but has it really told you anything of a "positive" nature? So far in my encounters I have not yet been told anything that I didn't already know! And I am very serious in my searching and seeking!

So who is going to tell me what I and probably others want to know? Some people will say. "Well perhaps we are not meant to know"! Yet as we shall eventually be upon that dimension of true reality, the more we know of what awaits us, the better prepared mentally we should be!!

But then! Am I not looking at this from a physical point of view? When I've already written that we, that is "our Spirit self" have already lived upon that sphere of the Spirit and know about it and it's procedures!! So in fact I should already know the answers to the questions I'm posing!!! And how do I get to know these things that I already know but as yet have no knowledge of, or perhaps I should have said "No recollection of"!! which I feel is more apt!!! so how do "I" the physical me get in touch with "Me" the Spirit partner of this my lifespan upon earth??! Do we get hidden information via our subconscious or through intuition? Or through the voice of someone else? A Teacher maybe! Or then again through the written word on a page in a book!!! Whether Ancient! Or Modern! If we look at everything that we are studying with an "open mind" and sift through what we have discovered "a truth" may very well present itself to you! And you notice I have said "A Truth" not "The Whole Truth"!! That will only be revealed to the searcher for it when they are ready to receive it, and that may take many, many, lifetimes and even then another facet of "The Truth" may allude you, who knows?!!

Even now I'm none the wiser than when I started this narrative, I suppose I'm really hoping for something like a bolt of lightning to strike me with Spiritual illumination! Perhaps truth is never revealed like that, maybe we already have it and something jogs our memory and we find another piece of the jigsaw fit's into it's allotted space, and that part of the picture of Truth shows us that we are on the right track, so we still have a long way to go before we actually see how the picture is taking shape!! Such a lot of talk and not much substance so far is there?

Now going back to those "areas" I mentioned. Perhaps that's where our Spirit goes to, for a form of assessment as to how far it's come regarding it's many incarnations! And perhaps those "examiners" will decide what is best for us, that is our Spirit Self. We maybe able to shall I say "skip an incarnation" if we are prepared to take the advice offered and do that incarnation on the Spirit area that we are upon. And because it would be our Spirit doing the learning itself and not needing a surrogate body to work through like upon the earth. That learning or incarnation could well be quite a brief one, but one that has helped us to progress more spiritually and so the next one upon earth could well be either the last one needing a physical body as host or the beginning of a much more Spiritual one, perhaps as a teacher or a mystic of a high order of Spirituality that can influence other's along the path of learning and there will come a teacher who may be of a very humble origins, so you will never know when if they contact you, they may not be quite what you expect, but look within and not at the seen face that you first observe, for that face can change even while you behold it, and the features may well be of one that has been known to many in the past!!!! Think upon that but do not speculate any further. Remember always with an open mind, and you will not go far wrong!! There is coming but not yet an age of great Spiritual awakening there will be many visitations from those upon the Higher Realms of the Spirit

World's, all round this World of yours and that means that ordinary people will unite with those of other continents. Minds will be uplifted, and no one Religion will be favoured above the rest. For Religion is but the scaffolding that for too long has obscured the Divine building that will now be seen. God in all of His Glory. Not covered in cloth of gold, but in homespun garment's of Truth. And here we speak Theoretically think upon what we have said to you and accept it if you can.

We leave you, your little scribe doesn't know what writing is his and what is our's never mind little friend it all stems from the one source, including your own!!

Peace we leave with you from this day forward.

Farewell and God's blessing's be upon and within you all.

Farewell.

Chapter 20

September 5th 2004

REMEMBERING?

One or two of us were talking about the physical body and it's relationship with the Spirit and some one said "Well what about when you half remember things that happened to you in a previous life, does that mean that you this physical you have lived before in a previous incarnation?" and that made me think, because I too have had not exactly remembrances of a past existences but I did have a sort of encounter during one night and when I asked the person who he was, he laughed and said "You! At least I used to be"!! There was more, and it ended with him saying "I don't think we shall meet again" and that was the end of that encounter. I felt a bit sorry and would liked to have known more about this previous Me!

But now, since I've been thinking about things I've wondered "It" could not have been me that is this physical me, for once the body has ceased to exist, that then is the end of this ones incarnation isn't it? Body, no longer viable for the Spirit to use!! So! Was that encounter that I had really to do with the Spirits memory of what happened in that particular incarnation? For the physical body that it was using at that time would have died and have been no more, but could have "lived" as it were in the memory bank of my Spirit!!!

I don't think it's possible for each incarnated being to have also actually lived before, because this human body is only temporary one for the use of the Spirit, who it seems is not affected by death in any way, for it is Eternal, just like the Creator who first gave it the breath of everlasting life!!! So are those memories of the Spirit stored somewhere, like a pack of cards, that can be taken out and looked at for various reasons, and just for a while that particular "card" becomes shall I say "alive once more". And perhaps if it is the Spirit who is doing the viewing it might allow "me" in this particular incarnation to also "see" this previous one who has contributed to my life in one way or another?!! Well now that I think about it, it does make sense and is quite logical as far as I can see! For after all it is my Spirit that is now a part of me, who has had to come to earth to learn about who it really is!! And I suppose at the end of it's necessary incarnations we the physical bodies that it has used are part of it's sum total of experiences that it needed in it's upward journey back to it's Divine source!!! I wonder if sometimes when my Spirit and that includes all people's Spirits, I wonder if it takes out this pack of memory cards and places them in sequence to see how He, that is the Spirit has progressed so far, and what more if any, will it need in further incarnations? And does it perhaps have a preference for a particular form of identity, and so chooses a body that has similar qualifications to a previous one, that he "the Spirit" was comfortable with during that particular incarnation?!!!

That could perhaps account for the feeling we sometimes get that "this" has all happened before to us, but we can't remember where or when!!! But it really hasn't been to us personally but to one of our shall I call them, "our ancestor's"!!! Gowing a bit further along that line of discovery, perhaps our Spirit has allowed part of it's memory bank to be part of "our" physical memory bank to help us in this present life with perhaps certain qualities that "it" feel's could be advantageous to us, maybe in the artistic sense, or the inventive frame of mind in fact almost anything you care to mention!

That could account for the fact that certain things seem to come very easily to a person, and looking back at the present families antecedent's there is no history of what perhaps this ones abilities can be traced to!!! Always I feel that logic comes into all that perhaps at first seems unaccountable, but when you know the answer then everything fall's into place!!!

So perhaps we need to study ourselves more closely, not only in our relationship with our Spirit partner, but also with those of the past, that have been the reason for us being who, and where we are!! But that part of trying to discover is certainly not easy. Perhaps in our deep dream state we may be able to come up with some of the answers, but there again trying to remember "deep dreams" is not as easy as saying it is, is it? But if we really are sincere in our efforts, I'm sure it will get easier in time!!!

It's really knowing and accepting who you now are and building upon that, you are just a temporary dwelling place for the real you, you matter and you are necessary and what you the physical body achieves helps the Spirit you in it's progression. So you are doing it for yourself really aren't you? And if you can look at it in that light it should help you in the living of this part of your ongoing life.

Your Spirit can look back upon this incarnation as a very worthwhile and satisfactory one and that should give you, the physical great comfort.

Chapter 21

September 7th 2004

SPACE AND THE UNIVERSE

Logic! Logic! Logic! Our whole world is based upon logic, as is the Universe that houses it! And beyond? Now that is something that the scientific bodies do not delve into too deeply, for they have no knowledge of what lies beyond the seen perimeter of this Universe!! Have they not thought that though we talk of "Space" as if it is the unseen substance that lies within the Universe's boundaries, that the Universe itself must also dwell in "Space" which is beyond what we can see! And going still further can there not be other so called Universe's circling perhaps like giant planets in Space, that is not visible and yet is everywhere, for without the nothingness of space, life would come to an end. And a very sticky one at that!!!

So that is where Logic comes in, for everything seen or unseen that has been created and is still being so, must be based on Logic! What may seem to have come about by chance as it were, has not been, looked at from a logical point of view!! Nothing gets created by "chance". If it does then it is from "mutation" and even that is governed by "laws" that are aspects of that Logic we keep repeating!! Logic is another form of mathematical equation! And that immediately say's a Mind must be at the back of it!! A mind so vast and complex that it is somewhat like the honeycomb of the bees!! Each cell complete in itself and yet all part of the overall structure of the hive!

That then is the Mind substance of the Supreme Creator of all that there is. And each one of these little cells, represent another facet of that creation. And these cells in turn contain the nucleus of an unborn creator!!! In their embryonic stage! Waiting for the Breath of Life to be instilled within their breast!!! This all must be looked at from a hypothetical viewpoint for to verify such a complex condition is simply impossible as far as Mankind is concerned!! Upon those Higher Spheres where light emanations hide the true identity of those "Beings of Light" that have never strayed from those Spheres governed entirely by the Mind substance of the Creator of all creators!!! And that word Creator covers a vast area of what cannot be understood by the lay person!! For creation forever undergoes "change" it does not "die" in the sense that you upon earth think of that word, which in actual fact only applies to the earth plane and nowhere else in the Cosmos!!!

The word "change" is its only equivalent and it does not mean death but re-orientation! What is today may not be the same tomorrow. Theoretically speaking just remember that everything is ordered, yes even "chaos" strange as that may seem!! When "things" are happening around you it is difficult to view them with equanimity!! So the only way out of that dilemma is to use your mind and find the correct solution that is applicable to the situation! And afterwards when comparative peace is once more restored, then you can start to question as to where all this Logic can be applied, and it may well surprise you that you will find that it does! But maybe not in the way that you think!!!

We have to "grow up" in the way we understand how this World, this earth, this Universe, and even ourselves are all part of a vast thought out scheme that really is perhaps beyond us at present. We have been programmed up to a point, but then we have our freedom of will, that is a divine gift if only we learn to use it properly. And that means in our attitudes towards the other members of our species!! Which most of us fail to do. Hence the Wars, and the lack of feeling towards those people of the poorer nations!! We have stressed before about the re-distribution of even the basic commodities that can mean all the difference between life and death, and here we are going to repeat that word "Logic" for is it not "logical" that all peoples all over your world should be free from hunger and starvation and then you would be free from War and disease and Harmony would reign where evil does at present!

Other planets have overcome these evils and if they can so can you!! It will require discipline on the part of all peoples, but it will be worth it. But do not leave it until it is too late. For tomorrow is just around the corner and you know not what tomorrow may bring!!!

We bid you Farewell, think upon what we have said and you will know that it makes sense!

Farewell Brother Scribe, Farewell. Peace be with you.

Chapter 22

September 8th 2004

THE SPIRIT WORLD IS A TRUE REALITY

I sometimes wonder if we don't expect too much from those upon the Spirit plane. For one thing they are not infallible and then again we should not expect them to how can I put it? We should not expect them to be at our beck and call! We are told that our loved ones are but a "thought away". All very comforting, and that may be the case in theory, but in practical terms I feel it may be quite different!! Looking at it from a logical point of view, they, that is our loved ones who perhaps have been upon the Spirit plane for a considerable time, have their own lives to be getting on with and that does not include popping back and forth when we send out thought messages, hoping that somehow they will let us know of their presence!! Is that really fair do you think? And then we know that they are now a Spirit form, which does not exactly tally with the physical body that we remember them by!

Now this may upset some people when they read this, because in a way they expect the loved one to remain as they want them to, which of course is not the case, for that would be hindering their progress wouldn't it? And also that would be perhaps selfish on our part, had you thought of it in that way? I admit it's only natural to somehow want to cling onto those loved ones, but they are in another dimension now, not in ours, and working within the laws of the Spirit realm they can't just "drop everything" so to speak, because we may be sending out a distress signal!! I am not being unkind when I say that, but I feel we must try and change our attitudes regarding not only our loved ones but the whole Spirit world in general!

It really is not this airy fairy world that so many people seem to think it is! It is a very practical and shall I say "a down to earth" realm, where you continue your journey of life, not quite as you have been doing upon earth, for you are now your true self, your Spirit self, which is not at all like the physical one you used to be!! Most people when they think of the next world are thinking of it with their physical senses, and of course that means they are not thinking straight. In a way they want this illusion that they have of the Spirit world to be a reality a reality of their own making!! Well I'm afraid it isn't? Certainly it is a Reality but it is a Spirit Reality and not a replica of the earth one!! If it was, then what would be the point of transferring from one sphere to another? No, dear friends you must be prepared to alter your former thoughts on that subject! It really is for your own good you know. If you accept that the world of the Spirit is the next stepping stone upon the upward path of your evolution then you will know that it must inevitability be different from the last one that was your physical one upon the earth!

Now some of you will ask about the loved ones that we long to be reunited with, and you will say "I want them to be as I remember them, not some Spirit form that I don't recognise"!! That is quite understandable but you are thinking in terms of "I want", and not what is the reality of becoming a Spirit and all that that entails!

But here we can tell you that all is not lost. When you as Spirit arrive or shall we say awake upon the Spirit plane, you are virtually the same to look at, as you have been, you don't feel any different and that is because your Spirit has taken on the garb of the physical for a set period, and that is all to make you feel comfortable in your new surrounding's. And now we come to your loved ones and friends! Yes! You do see them as you remember them, for they have the ability to assume that likeness for as long as it is suitable, that is for your benefit. Gradually though they will change back to their true Spiritual likeness, just as you are changing, without actually being aware of it! Your mental state is also changing, the remembrances of the earth are beginning to fade into a form of dream like past. You are adjusting to this new life style, as spirit you do remember your previous "visits" to this plane of Thought. Soon you will be able to function entirely as a Spirit, and then your new round of experiences await you, for you have still quite a lot to learn about this your new life and what is expected of you!! Don't be daunted by that word "expected of you"! For you are now far more capable than you realise!! You will be shown how you can project your image without actually leaving the spot you are upon!! This image is a form of "living hologram" or you might say a "clone" of who you are now!! That is when you wish to be somewhere else and yet remain in essence where you are!! This form of transference is what many Spirits use when they contact the earth plane if for instance at a clairvoyant meeting! They are to all intents and purposes who they are or if required who they were. You cannot tell the difference for they behave exactly as they have always behaved!! And when the visitation is over they are withdrawn by thought, back, to the one who created by thought, this other being! There is much more regarding this thought transference, for the possibilities are endless when you are proficient in this enterprise. But this is a serious subject and not one to be taken lightly, and here we are speaking of those upon the realm of the Spirit.

One day you too will be here upon this Realm of Realization, which shows you just what you are capable of. The life that awaits you is full of surprises, but remember you do not perform miraculous feats! There are guidelines and laws which it is your duty to abide by and happily most people are only to anxious to do so!

Before we go we feel that there is one thing that people feel uneasy about, and that is this feeling of having been here before and here we are talking of the earth plane not the Spirit. And yet they know that the physical body only lasts for one lifetime. Well there is an explanation for this. Sometimes a Spirit gets very attached to a certain family and when one incarnation has finished and in the course of time when it, the Spirit needs a further incarnation it chooses another member of that same family if one exists. And so that one can sometimes feel that they have been here before because they can remember places and events and it puzzles them. The reason being is that they are part of that families shared memories and so things are familiar even if perhaps a century or more has passed since those memories were a reality!! And all of these shared memories have been carried over by the Spirit now incarnating in that physical body of today.

Does that explanation help to throw a light upon what to some people has been perplexing them? As you can see there's such a lot about Spirit and the world that it inhabits that those upon the earth plane ought to know about, but we feel that we must leave that discussion for a future date! And so we bid you Farewell dear friends upon the Earth and to the little scribe. Farewell dear friend, Farewell.

Chapter 23

September 9th 2004

WE ARE MORE THAN WE THINK WE ARE

Think not of yourself as just another human being. For you are more complex than that phrase implies! You are a many faceted creature of likes and dislikes, and more importantly of character changes, that were somebody to show you just how many sides you have to your character you may well be astonished and probably not believe them and say they are exaggerating for you only have one character as far as you are concerned!! But just think about it for awhile and you will realise that you do not show the same side of your character to everyone, even if you have always thought that you do! For the character that is us cannot be seen as it were with the naked eye! And yet it is an essential part of our physical makeup!! Character is formed as we grow from childhood to maturity and beyond!! It stems from our attitude's towards everything that crosses our path in this lifetime upon earth, and yes even upon the Spirit realm our character still grows! But there, we are more aware of how it affects others, something that we don't always take into consideration upon the earth plane! More's the pity! But then as I have said we are not always aware that we don't show all of our character at all times! And that means we only show a part of it, that part, that without knowing it we unconsciously separate from the whole as it were. The part that a particular person of our acquaintance shall we say, is used to seeing!! So even if character can only be observed but not actually seen, for instance like an arm or a leg. It never the less is a visible part of us, and we can't get away from it!! So to one we may appear quite placid, and never get flustered but to someone else we may appear quite the opposite depending upon the situation!! And that is just two sides and there are many more when you begin to think about it. So now do you accept what has been said so far? I expect you'll say "yes! But with reservation"! It really is others who "see" our character isn't it, we are hardly in a position to judge our character for ourselves are we? We can judge other peoples and probably we do, but ourselves? No! I don't think that's possible unless a kind friend points it out to us!! Well now just go a step further and consider your other "bodies" that go to make you who you are!! You will probably say "What bodies? Where are they, I haven't seen them"!! No, most likely you haven't, but they do exist even if they can't be seen unless you are a clairvoyant! Some of them do have this ability, and it's all to do with your "Aura". And the vibrations that emanate from your conscious body that you can sometimes feel but not quite understand! When you feel "on top of the world" you radiate a glow of vitality that other people are conscious of, likewise when you are feeling "out of Sorts", your vitality has ebbed, you look and feel low!!! Usually we just accept these good and bad days without a great deal of thought, but the "bad ones" can be minimised if you want them to. And that is by withdrawing yourself literally to a place that is quiet and free from noise, close your eyes, and breathe deeply, and let all of those things that are upsetting you flow right out of your body, and when "they" get to your feet, stamp on them, let them know that you are the master and not them. Then take a few more deep breath's move your hands right from the top of your head and down your body in a sweeping motion, and now you can face the world once more, and you'll feel better for this little exercise in thought power!!

Now then what about those other "you" that you really do not know about, the ones that dwell upon the higher planes of the

Spirit. You might say that they are reflections of you not of your physical appearance but of your Spirit self. They may even just be a form of Spirit essence, awaiting the time when "you" may need them on your journey back "home". They have been created by your "Soul mind" just in case they are needed they are still part of you but on a higher spiritual level. They can influence you in a way, with higher thoughts and ideals, and you may wonder where these thoughts have come from, they are from you, but have laid dormant until the right time, your guiding Spirit, the one that is part of your earth body has been in contact with them and so those higher thoughts are given to you via that one that is nearest to you. You see we are a very complex form of humanity are we not? And the more we know about our "true self" the easier life becomes, both here and on the Spirit World. When some of those Higher you can be in contact with you on a more "personal level". And as you progress higher so you shed these other garments that clothe you until once more you are united with your Soul essence, and then begins the final journey of the Soul with all of the knowledge that "all of you" have gathered for it, the reason that the Soul was first created to understand it's relationship with the Divine Creator. And here I feel is where I had better end this writing for I cannot know what lies beyond the Soul plane, even if I would dearly like to know, but I realize that, that, information is beyond my feeble reasoning!!!

And so this is where I will end. And say to you Farewell!!

Chapter 24

September 11th 2004 2.40 a.m.

RELIGION! WHAT RELIGION?!

Religion!! What an emotive word! Why is it that when people start to discuss religion they become not only possessive of that word but somewhat aggressive as well! They seem to feel that they have got to somehow "stand up" for what they say they believe in, and they become very suspicious of anyone who perhaps voices doubts about either their particular Religion or even religion in general!! And what does that word really mean? It means everything and anything to whoever it is that is expressing what they say they believe in!! "It", that is religion is supposed to be all about God! But with so many variations on that subject, you could be forgiven if you were to think that none of them are speaking about the One God but many!!

Well does that really matter if it is what a certain group of people wish to identify themselves with? But do they even attempt to practise what they preach? Quite honestly very few really even understand the basic principles of their particular brand of Religious culture! They pay a form of lip service to it and that is about all they really do!! Some dress up their religious beliefs with all sorts of rituals that have absolutely nothing to do with what that word Religion is supposed to represent. Most of what they do is a form of "showing off" to others that their faith is the true one and all others are but pale replicas of it!! Have they really understood that what they are practising is merely their way of telling God that they want Him to know how they feel about Him, and hope that He feels the same way about them!!

Do they honestly think that God is as small as that? To be confined to one sect and ignore all others? Religion is Man made, and NOT God's!! Man has invented that form of entreating the Almighty with all of his wants and desires, all what he wants and nothing of what God wants or even expects!! Man has written a set of guide lines and forms of ritualistic postures not for God's benefit but to satisfy his own inadequacy. Just a lot of show and for whose benefit? Why his own and those who care to follow his example!! God does not need or even request all of this so called adoration, it's the simple things of life that are the pleasures that please Goad. And by simple pleasures we mean giving to others, Love and understanding binding up the wounds that words and deeds have been inflicted upon others, who perhaps do not see God in the same light as you do!!

God the Creator is beyond all the petty squabbling of Man in his attempt to show to others that what he believes in, should also be the belief of others!!! Sadly this can never come about, all the time that Man shows his intolerance of his fellow man by insisting that His way is the only way. Has he, that is man, received God's sanction for that kind of behaviour? No! No! No! in spite of what he may have read in ancient manuscripts, which after all were written by Man and not by God personally!!!

Man has been told that he was made in the image of God, and it seems he never tires of telling God about it!! But why then doesn't Man try to act as he knows the Almighty would wish him to? No! Man speaks, but his actions tell another story! And why? Is it because he is basically unsure of himself, and he thinks that force is the only answer to cover up his feelings of insecurity? Force is never the answer, for when you force someone to behave as you think they should, they will ultimately rebel against this enforcement and that is how your war's start!! And continue and become a sore that refuses to heal!!!

When man accepts that God is the God of all peoples, regardless of what name you choose to call him by, for God's name is Nameless or if you have to give Him an identifiable name then just call Him the God of Love the universal love that knows No boundaries of race creed or culture! You have been created by Love and through Love so why not try and live by Love? It's the only answer that can bring peace and security to one and all.

God does not ask for your adoration just your love, and that, by expressing it to your fellow man, for that shows God that you do understand what he is all about. For Love should be the Religion that you can live by, that really is what Religion should be, for Love, true Universal love fulfils all of God's wishes for His children of the earth. By expressing that, by deeds of Love you really are an image of the One on High. Be true to yourself and that means be true to God, Look upon your neighbour as your Brother and not as a stranger to be avoided. When man accepts that he is part of a world wide family of human beings that are God created, then he can show his Love for God by loving them. Then truly we can say "We are made in the Image of God our Father". That is the only Religion you need to practice, the simple answer to all of life's problems.

Turn back to God you do not need a religion to tell you that, for the God spirit that dwells within you is all that is needed for you to become what you were meant to be. A child of God, in His image you were created, believe that and go forward with His blessing's. Love your fellow man and let that be the Religion that really would be what God could be proud of, and man also!!

We bid you Farewell and leave you with God's blessing's that come with His and our Love.

And to you little Brother Our Love and our blessings for now and the future. Farewell, Farewell, Farewell!

Chapter 25

September 15th 2004

HYPOTHETICAL THOUGHTS!

Thoughts!

I've just thought about the Universe! Thinking about space and that this Universe of "ours" must be in some way "floating" in it. That means that there must be an "outside" to this Universe as well as what we see and are a part of "the inside". So! Could we go through the Universe and come out the other side I wonder? And if that is possible and of course this is all Hypothetical on my part, could it be that there are other worlds and planets etc vibrating and alive and we know nothing of them! And this has just occurred to me if we could go "through" that means "they" whoever "they" are could well come through to "our side"!!!

Now that opens up a completely new avenue of thought doesn't it? Perhaps "some" of what is on our side could "slip through" and then even return at a later date!!! That all sounds like fiction writing doesn't it? But could that be the answer regarding "Black Holes"? for if they go through what the Universe is made of then they must end up somewhere mustn't they? All very confusing but rather exciting when you think about it! Just imagine a parallel Universe!! And all that it might contain!!! Looking at it like that who knows, this World of ours may find itself orbiting on the other side one day!!!

And then Space being what it is, it could well contain a series of Universes, and this could be never ending! Now supposing that Space is not this empty nothingness that we think it is! Supposing it is actually a vibrating living invisible substance, that contains all the ingredients for the making of Worlds, planets, etc, that lie dormant until A "Creator" uses those ingredients or some of them for that very purpose? And who and what would that "Creator" be? A "Mind Essence"? that is a form of Untapped Electricity so vast as to be incomprehensible to our thinking? An essence capable of fusing together in correct order what constitutes a planet, a world, a galaxy, that once formed in its original state can go on to form other replica's of itself with all of this left over debris that seems to float about in uncertain ways!!!

That sort of implies that a World or planet has some sort of mind activity of it's own, which has been endowed within it, by that original Creative Source!!! And are there many of these Creators of "Creative" "source or force", and do "they" ever come together for a particular reason? All very speculative on my part, no doubt!! And probably bearing no relation to what might be the Truth!!

So that also means that we must look at "Our God" in a different light doesn't it? He, that is Our God, can't be the one responsible for all of this vast Creation of Cosmic endeavour!! For if "He" was, then he couldn't possibly be of a Human like stature could he? I feel He is the Creator of all that is in our World, but not what is outside of it!! And even then I feel he also delegates certain aspects of creation to others who are in the "Hierarchy of Creativity"!!! I expect most people will think I'm being heretical but I don't mean to offend anybody it's just my thinking and really just for myself to try and reason out what probably is really impossible for me, with my limited intelligence at present!!!

But the whole concept of Creation, that is the Universe and what it holds is such a vast subject that I don't think Mankind has been programmed to delve too deeply into those unknown areas of the hidden mysteries of Creation and those who do the Creating!!!

Which brings me to this. I believe that there is ONE CREATOR above all others, and those others being a Hierarchy of 12 separate Creators in their own right. Now these others are nothing to do with the various God's that are also Creators in their own right. But they create all of the living animate and inanimate creations that go to make up a World or Planet. And so we have what we have always had and understood as our God. Nothing has changed in that respect, He is our Creator, and we are one of His many Creations. And so we, shall I say, owe our allegiance to "Him" and "Him" only. I'm mot sure if there are many separate Gods that have jurisdiction over various Worlds and Planets, but I somehow think that there must be. I think Our God is also responsible for what we term the "Spirit World" which we are told is the Real World, and not this Earthly one which is a teaching and training world that helps to fit us for the one we have called "The Real World". So it would seem that "that one" is the really important one as opposed to this Earth one that most people think is the important one, mainly because they actually physically live upon it, and the other one, the Spirit one is one they are not sure about, because they can't actually "see" it and have to take on trust when someone tells them it really does exist and that we all go there after our brief life span has reached its allotted time!!! And though we as a physical human being cease to exist this Earth World does continue to do so! But our Spirit counterpart that has been the guiding force in our earthly life continues and never dies, alters yes, but does not die! So it is the Spirit then that is the real one that was created by God and the physical human being as it were, is a bi-product that has been created for our, the Spirit's use when it has to incarnate upon the Earth for learning experiences that help it in its evolutionary progress!

So though for a while we the human side of the Spirit are shall we say the important one while we live, and when our body relinquishes the life force we no longer exist as a human body. We have as it were been absorbed into the Spirit, with all our thoughts and memories and so in a way we have not died for we are a necessary part of the Spirit and always will be. For memory which is a strong thought aspect of the mind continues within the confines of the Spirit essence or body if that is how you still wish to identify yourself as. And it would seem that to most people they feel that they still continue to be a body that is recognisable as who they have always been. Which in a way is correct, except that the human physical part, the shell that encased the real you is no longer required when the Spirit once more returns to the world of the Spirit, but you are still you and will continue to remain so until the Spirit leaves behind all of those memories of the Earth plane that have contributed to its present phase in its upward spiral of evolvement!! And so that lifespan that you the physical lived is now just a memory and you now go on with this your new life as Spirit You. We change we alter, we have experienced that time upon Earth and it is part of us now, but we must go on, and leave that period of learning behind us.

We may even once more incarnate back upon Earth if we , our Spirit feels it is necessary, and then our Spirit will choose once more as suitable physical human being to be its companion for another lifespan of that human being, and so the wheel of life continues, and so once more you the Spirit are again within a physical human body for further knowledge and experience. Your life begins afresh and once again you and your physical body will once more be joined together and so memories of this life will be added to all of those others that have made You the Spirit who you are!! A Spirit and now once again in human disguise!! Will this we wonder be the last of the human companions that the Spirit needs in its development?

Perhaps this is where this discourse should end. And so this is where is does!!

Chapter 26

September 22nd 2004 2.00 a.m.

DO WE REALLY UNDERSTAND GOD?

What exactly is our relationship with God? And here I stress the word God and not the Creator of all that we think of as the Cosmos and the beyond!! I feel that for too long we have not really given God the "thinking" that we should. We often accept the traditional teaching about God, but we don't really think of what those thoughts actually mean!!! Is it because if we did stop and think deeply we might be in for quite a shock!! That is our ego I am talking about! For as long as we just keep on saying "God the Father" and leave it at that we perhaps feel that is sufficient! But is it? If you are a thinking person, you want to know more about the one we call God!! Who is "He"? Where is "He"? and what is "He"?!!!

If you think about the Universe and what it contains, which we seem to know precious little about, you have to re-think your cosy thoughts of the God of tradition!!! And more importantly what is our relationship towards Him!!! We are such small creatures if you think about it, in comparison to the Universe that we perceive with our eyes!! And we don't even see a fraction of what is "out there" and all around us!! God created it all, and if that is correct do you really think that we small and insignificant as we are, can possibly know all that there is to know about the being we call God? We cannot equate Him as a "human like being". "He" is too vast to bring Him down to our size, or one that we could feel comfortable with if we were to suddenly be confronted by Him!!! We are brought up with stories from the Bible relating to God and those ancient figures of the past, but did that really happen? Or is it Man's idea of what might have taken place, the idea that God is like a benign Father figure sometimes good and sometimes not so good when we offend him in some way!!!

Just stop! And really think, could that have possibly happened in a real sense, or is it Man's feeble attempt to try and come to terms with things that are too vast for him to understand with any accuracy?!!! If we go on thinking like we have been brought up to think, then we will never get any where near the truth of what and who God really is!!!

I feel, and it is only how I think, that the one we call God is our God, our Creator, but is not the Creator of the Universe and beyond. That One must be of a completely different order of Being!! One so vast as to be utterly incomprehensible to mankind in his present state of learning and understanding!!! The utter power of a Mind capable of such creation is so staggering that we couldn't even begin to try and come to terms with it, and if we did, then I think we would drive ourselves insane!!! That form of creative activity must always remain a mystery to us. We are permitted to see our God as we want to, and that is for our own good and satisfaction! It allows us to feel comfortable if that is the right word, when we think and talk about Him!!!

He is our creator the one who created us and what we can see when we look around our World. And that should be sufficient for us in our present state of evolution!! We are, it seems to me still in a fairly primitive stage in this cycle of evolvement!! Just think of all the wondrous things that have been created, man included upon and within this World of ours!! Just trying to understand that part of creation taxes our minds doesn't it? So how can we come to terms with what has been created outside of our World's orbit? Is our God responsible for that? Or are there other Beings of like stature that have that responsibitlty?! I feel our minds are somewhat blinkered when we start thinking about "what goes on" out there in this vastness of the Universe!! Our scientists try to understand, but they are limited in their endeavours when you think in terms of millions and millions of miles that make up space and the term "light years away" that then takes us back in time even further!!! Who controls this vastness? And more to the point who keeps is under control?!!

When you start to think along those lines you begin to realize how small and insignificant Man really is in comparison!! Can you really visualize us as being on personal speaking terms with a Being who is responsible for all of that?!! I feel we have such a lot of rethinking to do if we want to try and understand what God is all about, and how we fit into the scheme of things, and that only goes for the physical side of who we are. When you start to think about our Spirit the real one of who we are, we then have to enter into another dimension of learning! For that world, though our real home so to speak is one that we as yet do not know a great deal about. I wonder why? For we are told that it is the real and permanent place of existence that we all go to, when the mortal body ceases to function upon the Earth plane!! Perhaps if we try and understand our Spirit side more, and try to be in tune with it we would be given further insight into that sphere that seems so tantalizing when we talk of the World of the Spirit!!

And that world is another aspect of our Creator is it not? And that one is the one to which we belong for as Spirit that is our permanent dwelling place, not like this material world, which we only inhabit for a brief period of time as a physical human being, and once we die then that body is of no further use to our Spirit is it? So why are we not in more communion with it? Or perhaps we are and we don't realize it, at least not all of the time!! And when we do start to appreciate our other self, then perhaps we are travelling on the upward path of realization, where we meet others of a like mind. Fellow travellers upon that path that leads us back to the source of Divine Creation. And now we can say goodbye to our Earth life for it has served its purpose in awakening our "Spirit

Consciousness", which is why we came to Earth to find, in the first place. Our Spirit, now released from it bondage of the mortal body it can now be its true self once more. Lessons learned, and a new life beginning where we truly belong upon "The Spirit World" of reality. The one that will lead us back to our God and salvation!! Now, knowing who we are and why we are, who we are!!! We are Spirit in its purest essence, part of the Godhead, as we have always been, but not knowing it until Now! Journeys end, a new beginning beckons. And where will that lead to?? That then must be the start of another story yet to be written in this book of Life!!

So I will bring this chapter to a close and perhaps in time someone will enlighten me, till then it is now my turn to say Farewell.

Chapter 27

September 29th 2004

REALITY/ILLUSION ARE THEY ONE?

We will speak to you of Reality, and its so called opposite Illusion. And you notice we have said "so called opposite"! For even that statement is open to contradiction! Are we beginning to confuse you? You see how things or words can quite often be open to different interpretations, all to do with the perception of the one who is doing the perceiving so to speak!!

Illusion upon the Realm of the Spirit is not the same as Illusion upon the Earth plane! There, the one who is doing the art of Illusion is out to deceive the eye, you call them magicians they perform those acts to amuse and astound you, and you marvel at the dexterity of their hands even when you are so close to them, you cannot see what is done to deceive your senses! And notice we have said "senses" and that means not only the eyes that you see with!! Does that make you think!! For senses can also be manipulated by one who is very proficient in his art, for it is an "art" and a very clever one, but one that can be used by those who are unscrupulous in their behaviour. And here we are talking about those people you call "confidence tricksters". But we will not deal with that darker side of the term "Illusion"!

Illusion as you would expect has many, many facets to it, and to create this illusion there has to be a certain amount of so called "reality" attached to it to be able to perform this sleight of hand.

For instance to suddenly produce from between cupped hands a white dove, that then flies off to a perch that awaits it and while you are watching that, lo and behold the magician has delivered another one from seemingly nowhere! They are what we have called the "realities" for without them, there could be no illusion could there? So you can now see that within Illusion there is a semblance of Reality and likewise in Reality there is often a semblance of Illusion!!

And here is where we will transfer our explanations to our world. The World of the Spirit That is a reality, but which to some would almost seem like an illusion. An illusion of the senses! And all because they themselves have to take someone else's word for it, they personally are not in the position to verify for themselves the actual reality of what that word Spirit represents!! We can tell you all sorts of things about

"our world" because we know and have experienced them, but you only have our word for it don't you?!! So it is left to you to either accept or reject what is told to you! Rather a dilemma for you isn't it? For you want to accept what in your searching you have come to believe in, but there's always that nagging doubt that makes you unsure of what perhaps some people will say to you that leaves you wondering, was that true or not?

Now this is all part of Your, shall we say, lessons to be learnt!! Only accept what to you yourself, strikes you as either being feasible or a truth that perhaps in some way verifies what you have previously been told by someone else!! It's all a matter of what you believe in that satisfies this longing for positive proof of the reality of the life that exists beyond the grave! For in truth it really does, and as you have reached this stage in your evolutionary progress, now is the time to put all those doubts behind you and put your trust (if it warrants it!) in those who you can consider are your teachers and fellow travellers upon this ever upward path of inner knowledge, that can if you are willing, awaken those senses that have lain dormant, just waiting, waiting for this moment of realization that Life is one glorious journey upon the path that leads back to the source of all Creation, the Godhead, not of Antiquity but of the Now!!!

Now we can talk to you about this life of yours to come, where Reality and Illusion are shall we say interchangeable and yet always remaining the same Reality!! Rather a paradox you feel. Perhaps it is, but never the less it is a truth. And you notice we have said a truth which implies that there is more than one truth, or perhaps we should say more than one side to a truth. For Truth never stands still it moves with the times! And yet always remains a basic Truth! Another enigma for you to try and unravel!! And that is where reality and illusion play their part!! Our life upon the Realms of the Spirit World are forever changing, you may be upon, say, one realm and yet with your inner perception you can also dwell at times upon another!! That perception could be termed an illusion of the reality that does exist in another dimension, a dimension of the Mind, for it is the Mind that is its own Creator of those two illusive aspects, illusion and reality!! You create your own illusion of reality in your thoughts, and then you gravitate to where that reality exists, in reality!!

Illusion upon the Spirit planes in never one of deceit, it is just another aspect of the reality that exists everywhere but not always perceived as such!! You learn and in the learning you accept, and in that acceptance you are that much nearer to the true reality of TRUTH, the truth of who you really are and who you can become, when you have reached that stage of Perfection that is no longer an Illusion but a Reality, in other words GOD in all of His Majesty!! Journeys end? But No, just the beginning, the beginning of the New beginning, where you are in partnership with the Creator of all that you perceive. You are, with the Eternal One in Eternity!!! Just another aspect of the NOW!!! Reality! And not Illusion.

And here is where we bid you children of the Earth plane Farewell.

And to the little person who has allowed us to use his thoughts in this exercise of the mind, we thank you and extend our hands in friendship. We will meet little friend, never fear, for you belong to us now!! Farewell and may God bless you.

Farewell.

Chapter 28

September 30th 2004 2.35 a.m.

BRING BACK GOD INTO YOUR EVERYDAY LIVING

There is at this present time in Man's evolution a great fascination of what is commonly known as the "After Life" or the "Spirit World" People can see on their television screens pictures of clairvoyant demonstration and the "audience", I cannot call them the "congregation" though they almost seem like one!! Seem to be counted in their hundreds and all hoping by the look of them for a message from a loved one who has "passed over" to the other side!!! Or perhaps some are just sceptical of the whole thing, and yet many of those sceptics came away feeling that perhaps there is something to all of this after all!!!

People it seems are searching for explanations regarding not only death, but the whole meaning of life, the world at present is in a very funny state, what was "right yesterday" today is seen as not so! Or that is what they think!! The values that they thought were permanent are now blown away with the wind, like the autumn leaves that fall to the ground, leaving the tree bare and gaunt!!! And that is how they now see their lives, so these demonstrations that they witness

Are a form of trying to come to terms with what they feel has in the past been to them unexplainable!!

People seem very conscious now of the fragility of life, one day all seems normal, and the next day a hurricane sweeps all that normality away and they are left bewildered and sometimes with nothing left of what was their life style, gone, in an instant! And "Why" they wonder, what is God doing about it? And does He even care anymore?!! Yet so much of this turmoil can be traced to Man's mismanagement of this Earth upon which he dwells!! But he prefers to blame Nature for these catastrophe's and not himself!! This then is the time when he seeks explanations and the organization known as "Spiritualism" seems to be the only one that offers him some sort of hope for the future. And mediums seem to be the one who offer hope on that score, they try to show that this physical life is not the only one that Man is capable of living. For they show that even when the body dies, the spirit what animated that body goes on living upon another dimension that we call the "Spirit World". But so little is really known about it, to many it is known by another name and that is "Heaven", the name that the Church, and here we say that in the broadest sense, tells us that we all go to when we die! But they never explain in layman's terms what "Heaven" is really like. They seem to hope that, that word will satisfy the curious seeker and they leave them to do the rest!!

So now we come back to the "Mediums", who to many people have replaced the so called church authorities!! Yet Spiritualism doesn't call itself a church but a way of life, that we should try to live by. They do have their buildings that are considered as a church by those who go to them, even when some of them are almost like an "upper room" that Jesus and his disciples used for their meetings!! Well the mediums endeavour to give evidence of the continuity of life after the physical body is left behind at death. For to mediums there is no such thing as "death" but a transition from one sphere to another!

More and more people are coming round to that realization and want to know what this other dimension is all about and more to the point how does it affect their loved ones who have made that transition and now find themselves living upon that sphere!!! Those mediums who are genuine clairvoyants can and do "get in touch" with those who are now on that other plane of existence. Their methods of "contact" are varied according to the individual. And when positive proof is given to one who is seeking and searching for that proof, then that one now knows that the loved one who has left this Earth plane is very much alive upon the other one. And when that is accepted then the ones who are "left behind" can go on with their lives knowing that the gap that was left when the loved one departed is no longer a "gap" for they are still around and know just what is happening even when they cannot be visibly seen as it were by those who are left! That is why those mediums who are the genuine ones, do such good work in showing that there is no death just an alteration in the way that we live when transition takes place!!

This is all to do with the "Natural laws of the Universe". And when we learn to accept them and live by them, in other words live a decent life, the sort of life that Jesus showed us is possible even by today's standards, but it means altering ones previous attitudes that often meant putting "self first" instead of others, its bringing back God into our everyday living, not by being pious and "holier that thou". But just by treating your neighbour as your brother and not a hostile enemy that you try to avoid!! We have been given this life and the one to come to enjoy and by living a life that is full of love for our fellow human beings, we are fulfilling Gods law and living as he intended us to live, in harmony, surely that can't be that hard to achieve if we really set our minds to it. We are not just a physical body but one of Spirit the same as God is. And as Spirit our life is forever, it changes and we change with it. That is what is so glorious about it all. Accept that principle of Universal Love and learn to live by it and you will find that life does have a meaning to it after all, whatever sphere you happen to be living on, makes no difference, Love is what makes it all worthwhile in every sense!! Be at peace with yourself and we say once again let GOD back into your everyday living and you will then truly be living life to the full and that includes the one to come!!! May the blessings of the One on High be with you now and forever. Farewell!!

Chapter 29

October 2nd 2004 4.30 a.m.

THE GOLDEN CHAIN

The Soul plane!! Beyond and below! And here we deal with the "below"!! Each plane or sphere of existence below the soul plane and culminating upon the lowest of these planes, the Earth!! We start though not with the earth plane but the one adjacent to the Soul plane, adjacent and yet part of it as are all planes in relation to each other!! They are separate, and yet they interpenetrate as it were, forming what can be called an "onion of experience" in other words, layer upon layer if you were able to peel them back with Earth representing the very core of this so called onion!! We say "layer upon layer", but in actuality they represent layers of perception!! In other words "Extensions of the Mind". Realities and yet appearing as Non realities to the lower senses!! And when we say lower think not of how you consider lower but think once again of perceptions! For planes of the Spirit are forever "fluctuating". They are planes that are "alive and breathing" just as those who inhabit them! And think not of "those" as human like entities, for they are more than that, they are the essence of pure spirit that has the capacity for creating whatever it wishes too, at any particular time of its existence and that existence extends right through those other spheres up to and including the Earth one! Which is the densest of all and so is the lowest rung on the Spiritual ladder of evolution!!

When Soul has been created and given its home or dwelling place upon the plane of the Soul it remains there, perfect in its essence, but unaware of that perfection. It is Mind untapped! Thought, waiting to be awakened to it potentiality. It is the aspect of the Creator that is made "visible". And when the Creator breathes upon its creation, "it" becomes a living breathing entity, capable of becoming a creator in its own right! Within the limitations of its "remit", in other words its partial programmed self!! With that God given gift of Free Will. And it is left to the soul to explore this freedom, and bring it under control? Which seems like a paradox but it is not!!!

Upon the Soul plane dwell the "Masters of the Soul" in other words the Teachers of that element of the Creator, and here they devote their energies to enlightening the soul essence to its responsibilities of creation!! It is a form of schooling showing soul the wonders of creation and how "it" can become a creator of Spirit essences that will enable it to understand its true potential that is to lead it back eventually to the Divine Creator that created it in the first place, to once more be a part of that Creator, but now knowing who it is, and why it was created originally, to become a living part of the Creator of all things, for Creating is the life blood of the Creator and as such never ceases in the flow of Creativity which now encompasses those Souls that it created for this very purpose of continuity!!!

Soul, now that it is aware of it potentials and here we have gone back to its home on the Soul plane, attempts to create what its teacher's have taught it that it is capable of!

And so figuratively speaking it starts its downward journey of the exploration of itself via these other spirit essences that it has created to dwell upon each plane that it has to explore! These "essences" remain in an "inactive state" of slumber until they are required to awaken, which is when the very lowest of these essences the one we call "Our Spirit" springs into life and animates the "connecting cord" that joins all of these essences, and that "cord" is a form of electrical current that carries "thought waves" from the Spirit "controller" upon the Earth plane, so that each Spiritual essence uses it portion of the mind substance to store what is being transmitted to it!! The Earth plane Spirit is the main one until it ceases to need a physical body in its exploration, when it has completed its final round of physical incarnations, it enters into the next Spiritual essence upon the plane above the one that adjoins the physical plane. And so gradually the Spirit that was the animator of the physical body is now in turn animated by its "next in line" spirit essence, and so this journey will continue through each sphere of perception until it reaches once more the Soul who is its creator!! And here all of the knowledge gleaned by each of those aspects that were created by the Soul can now be collated and put into place, ready for the Soul to start "its" journey back to its source!! And the lives that are to be lived by the Soul on those upper and Higher planes of existence. That we are not allowed to inform you of. For they are of such Pure Spiritual essence that defies any form of explanation that we could impart, even if we were allowed to!!!

One day we will tell you of the various "realms" that those essences, those aspects, of the soul dwell upon and how they are affected by the knowledge that is imparted to them by their other aspects that link each other in the golden chain of Spiritual evolution!! And here we feel it is time to bid you brethren of the Earth Farewell. And to the little scribe, Farewell Brother, Farewell.

Chapter 30

October 5th 2004 2.00 a.m.

TIME! WHAT IS IT?

I've been thinking about "Time" upon the Spirit World! We are given to understand that time as we know it upon the Earth plane is not the same as it is upon the Spirit Realm! The reason I'm writing this is because last night I found myself "talking out loud" regarding time, and one of the things I remember was "Time and Tide wait for no man" and that time, was not relevant regarding those who are in the Spirit World. They can manipulate it to suit themselves!! Which I'm not sure that I quite understand!! Because time surely must be a reality, because if you are at point A, and you want to get to point B regardless of the distance that must take up time of some sort mustn't it? You can't just say I'm here at A and now I want to be at B and you are!! Or can you be when you are Spirit? But even then, however short the distance between those two points, it must take "time" to cover it, and if you assume that the Spirit can "halt" time and then start it up again what's the point of that?!! Perhaps it only applies to what I might call distances that are "far" and so to manipulate time for oneself would be acceptable, providing of course that it didn't inconvenience another person!!!

We are told that on the Spirit World, the past, the present, and the future, are all one they are the NOW!!! And so time is not part of it!!! I think I can understand that in its broadest sense, but not in its "smaller" for want of a better word, its smaller or lesser sense which would seem to me to be hardly worth the effort! Though it has just occurred to me that perhaps "Time" is not always the same, perhaps there are "degrees" of it! There must be some sort of law that governs it, otherwise I can foresee chaos all over the place!!! Of course I'm only looking at if from a physical and material viewpoint, which means I'm really in no position to try and explain what to me and probably others is unexplainable in "human terms"!!!!

Perhaps the word "Time" is not the correct word for "it". We are governed by time because we use "clocks" which tick away the minutes and the hours that make up our day! But if there are no clocks then time would not be seen to exist would it? We would just have Night and Day. But as we do have clocks then night and day become acceptable to most people, except perhaps for those who do not work what to most people is the "normal working day". So their "time scale" would be quite different, their night maybe their day and their day would be their night!! So looking at it like that, we do sort of manipulate our time even upon Earth!

So perhaps its not so strange after all, regarding this Time business upon the Spirit realm!! I seem to remember someone saying that upon the Spirit World there is no night time, just daytime!! Now why should that be I wonder? I see no reason for them not to have a night time! Perhaps their form of night time is more like a time of what we call twilight, neither light nor dark, just a nice in between!!! As I'm sure they have a Sun, if not more than one!! So why not a moon and there again perhaps two or even more!!! And that could go for the Sun's as well, for we are told that the light upon the Spirit world is truly beautiful and nothing like ours upon Earth!!

And if there are Sun's and Moon's are they like the Spirit World invisible to our mortal eyes??!! I guess that as this other world Is on a higher vibrationary force than we are that could account for it!! But what may seem invisible to us, must be visible somewhere, for it is a reality and not one of the imagination!! Perhaps it's the Lower spheres that are the invisible ones to those of Higher

Vibrations, and they may sometimes wonder if they are told about us, that perhaps we are just figments of their imaginative qualities!!! It makes you wonder just what is reality and what is illusion!! Perhaps it's best not to delve too deeply into those things in case the reality of them could be quite a shock and we might find that what we have always thought of as real may not be after all!!! I think that, that is where I had better close this subject before I become so confused that I don't know how to tell the difference between reality and illusion!!!

Chapter 31

October 7th 2004 1.00 a.m.

WE BEGIN

The World of the Spirit! Our World and yours. In fact everyone's for it is the true world to which we all belong, and from which we originate and ultimately return to, this we have been programmed to do come what may. Our Spirit Self that is the original one the one that never dies for it is the very essence of the one Creator of all that there is. Some of us can trace our beginnings from the very mists of time itself and yes even beyond that very time, when the Earth plane was in its infancy and mankind had not yet set foot upon it!!!! You may think that if that is true then we must be so ancient that we would almost defy description! But the Spirit is ageless, time has no meaning for it, for Spirit is born anew with each and every incarnation that it feels is a necessary part of it's evolutionary progress!! We have long ceased to be part of the stream of so called humanity and yet we are very aware of what is happening upon this planet you call Earth!! We dwell not upon the sphere that you call the Spirit One, for there are many in the spiral of the evolutionary cycle of man's journey back to the source of his beginning!! Each Sphere more beautiful than the last, with a beauty that cannot be described in human terms! For those Spheres that are part of the Highest realm that man can aspire to are the dwelling places of the Ones known as the Creators of all that there is!!!

And this is where Creation begins and where it well ultimately

End when it's cycle has reached its perfection of understanding and acceptance of what it is!!! For creation is more than what that word implies. It is the primordial chaos of Life itself before it becomes what you see about you and call your Universe. It is Spirit in it's purest state, it is the seen and the unseen Body of the Creator of all the Creators that exist to do the bidding of that ONE!! Call them Gods, call them Celestial Beings of Love and Light, call them the true Hierarchy of the inner circle of all Wisdom and Knowledge, they are all of these and more!!! And cannot be perceived by even the Highest of what you may think of as the Angelic Hosts!! Yet their love for their creations is boundless as in the One above all others!! The body known as the physical is but one of their many creations that are their expressions of their Love for their Creator. That body that is known as Mankind is the outward shell that houses the true creation that is called Spirit for Spirit is the very essence from that primordial chaos known as the Life force. Not all Spirit entities can be traced back to that source, for Spirit is forever being created anew! And yet a memory sometimes lingers within even some of the Spirit's that are still being created and formed, a memory dim and almost forgotten of a past existence that was theirs when they were still but a thought in the mind of a Creator!! For thought is the prelude to creation of every thing that exists, whether upon your planet called Earth or one of the many others that abound in the confines of your known Universe!!! Remember that all of creation comes from that primordial chaos that we spoke of and so we are all a part of that substance, we are part of where we are, and so we affect and are affected by our very surroundings.

Spirit, when it is released from its physical shell is more aware of this tie between "it" and "its" place of habitation! And the link grows ever stronger as the Spirit retraces its journey on its upward spiral that you call evolution. When you as Spirit accept this then you know that your real journey back to the source that you originally came from, has begun. The journey is long and sometimes arduous and may take hundreds if not thousands of your so called years before you reach that ultimate goal, but you will reach it, for that is the divine spark that dwells within us that knows that it is part of that Creator whose name though nameless is who we call our God!! For that magnetic force that is our very life's essence is so strong that nothing can stop that final union with that Divine Spirit that we are part of and that is part of us!!! Spirit is who and what we really are, we never die, we change, we alter, we become another aspect, but we always remain the true spirit that was created originally. So if sometimes you feel that you partly remember a lifetime that was yours a long long time ago, accept it as true, for you are ageless and as those remembrances become clearer so will your life become also, for to you there was never a time when you were NOT. Think upon that and know that life is eternal and that life is you. Go forward and live as a physical being who knows that within that physical body dwells a Spirit who is the true You and always will be!!

We will end this night's discourse and say May you receive the Blessings of the One on High now and forever. And to the little Brother scribe, Farewell little one we give you our love and our blessings also. Farewell.

Chapter 32

October 7th 2004

MORE OBSERVATIONS OF THE SPIRIT

Further to the previous discourse on "Spirit". As we live upon a world that is made of physical matter, as we ourselves are and that is only because we could not survive unless we are a physical being of a dense form of substance! Yet within that dense shell of matter our Spirit does survive and prospers in it's search for the meaning of life and it's relationship to it!!

Spirit only uses the physical body as a temporary dwelling place. It does not necessarily remain "in" it all the time! It shall we say "comes and goes" but is linked to its physical body by what some people call a "Silver cord" which actually is more than a "cord" it is an Electrical wavelength, somewhat like an umbilical cord that joins a Mother and baby in the gestation period, but the one of the Spirit cannot be broken unless the Spirit desires it, and that usually occurs when death overtakes the mortal body, and it is of no further use to the Spirit in this incarnation!! You notice we say "this incarnation" which implies there have been others and yet more to come if considered necessary by the "Spirit animator"!!

So Spirit is intrinsically a part of the physical vehicle, yet not actually dependent upon it for it's evolutionary progress!! In fact it is the other way around. For without the Spirit attachment the mortal body would not exist! So you see the Spirit is the important one in this joining of the Spirit and the physical part of this partnership for it's life time upon the Earth plane, while the Spirit continues with it's permanent "life" upon the next dimension for as long as it considers it desirable!! The Spirit is a very flexible "being" in many ways. It can if it wishes be seen and observed as the physical vehicle that it uses as a form of habitation, but the word "physical" is a from of illusion and is not a "physical reality" in the sense that you know it! And yet to all appearances it is identical in every respect, which as we have stressed is but an "illusion" that it is capable of assuming for purpose's that it feels is necessary at a particular period! Here we are talking about the transitional period when the Spirit departs from the physical body!!

It retains in "thought form" all of the characteristics and shall we say "idiosyncrasies" of the mortal body it has left behind. That is why when there is "contact" with what is known as a "medium" that Spirit entity is virtually a living replica of it's former self that lived upon the earth plane and so is recognisable to those loved ones that have been left behind. Those memories of that life are reinacted for the benefit of authentic evidence that can be understood and verified by the loved one who is being given what is known as a clairvoyant reading"!! But you must remember that it is the Spirit of that one that passed through the veil of death and not the actual physical body that was known and loved while upon the Earth plane, yet it IS that very one that was known, it is just that it was the physical part of that duo that was observed with the physical senses even though the Spirit was ever present though not shall we say, observed by the physical senses such as sight and touch. But never the less could be observed by those inner senses of true love that is the bond that joins one soul to another.

We are Spirit and always will be for that is the part of God that he has given of Himself to us, to one day be reunited with Him, knowing who we have become because of His Love for us, and if we can just try while dwelling in a human body to release that Spirit consciousness and live a life that is a tribute to that Love that has been given so freely and with no restrictions. And if we can do the same to our fellow brethren, then this earth life will be worth living not only for the human body but also for the Spirit within.

We leave you in His Love and with His blessing. Little Brother you are indeed blessed, believe that for it is the Truth. We bid you all Farewell!

Chapter 33

October 8th 2004 1.00 a.m.

THAT OTHER YOU!

The end of our trilogy on Spirit and our relationship with it!!!

We have told you about the Spirit Now we shall tell you about the activities that spirit is capable of doing!! Spirit has the ability to do many things that would astonish you if you could see them! Spirit is an "essence" that can either be seen or not seen depending upon the situation. This ability that it has, is common to all who inhabit the Spirit World, for Spirit can be observed as solid, warm and vibrant, and yet can in an instant alter it's vibration so that it is no longer visible and yet it can remain in the same vicinity as if it were still a visible being!! Spirit is a being of light and can be observed by some as a small vibrating ball of light, that seems to dart around before your eyes. It is also a vaporous cloud, that swirls with an energy of life force!! Spirit is a phenomena, solid objects are no barrier to its movement for it can glide right through an object of solidity as if it were not there!!! It is capable of so many so called "feats" for spirit is indestructible and is unique!! And that dear friends is what you and I are, Spirit in its purest sense!! Part of the Creator that Divine Spirit that pervades all of known life forms, for without the spirit consciousness we would be inanimate, just waiting for that life force to bring the mortal body into activity.

Spirit is somewhat of a plastic like substance that can absorb all the surrounding elements if it so desires, and so it can leave an imprint of itself upon shall we say a building if the conditions are right, that is why certain building, rooms or houses can evoke in a person who may have physic tendencies a feeling, not always of apprehension but perhaps of unease!!!! The thought's that the Spirit originally created either of love or fear can remain in a memory form long, long after the Spirit has left the mortal body that it inhabited when it was earth bound!! Some people call it "haunting" but in actuality it goes beyond that and to try and explain we do not propose to deal with in this discourse!! There is much that is not known about Spirit and the world to which it belongs that to collate the findings of it would require many volumes!!! We, that is all of us are those Spirits that we talk of and the more we can learn about ourselves then the understanding of who we really are would become clearer and Spirit would be seen in it's true light, not something to be in awe of, but a very necessary part of our existence whether upon the physical plane or the one of the Spirit!! We belong, as it were to both worlds and one day they will be united and become as one dimension and this Earth will no longer be one of dense matter but one of spiritual reality and so Spirit and physical will also be as one body True Spirit in every sense of the word. But that day, dear earth friends is a long way off we have to tell you. But that should not stop you from trying to find out just a little more about your other self, the real you, the spirit you. For that is the one that never dies, it never has, and never will, for it is the immortal part of us that is a part of our Creator God and so our life will go on and on until once more we are reunited with the source of all life and creation with our Father in Heaven.

We leave you there dear friends, with the blessing's of the One on High, Farewell! And to you little scribe of the night farewell and god bless you.

Chapter 34

October 9th 2004

THE UNION!

What is our true relationship with our Spirit Self? And here we are talking about the physical body, that the Spirit inhabits for that brief span that is called a lifetime!! The physical body, when it is aware of itself, by which we mean that it knows that it is more than the body that it sees as a reflection in a looking glass, it is then that this union becomes a living reality! Sadly though not all of us seem to be aware that behind that façade that we call "Self" there dwells a more important aspect of that "Self". The one that is not seen but nevertheless is an active part of the physical vehicle while it dwells upon the Earth plane. It is through this vehicle that spirit learns the lessons that it knows it needs and why it is incarnating in that mortal body, for that is the only way that it can learn the lessons that apply only to the lower sphere of Earth, and yet they influence those higher realms of the Spirit. So you can see that while the physical body lives, it is to all intents and purposes the main one, the important one, the one that Spirit in it's wisdom has itself chosen for the very purpose of it's learning!! It is a form of an "observer" and yet it also participates in the life of its human host!! That is to say that there are times when the Spirit can see "ahead" when perhaps the physical body is about to make a very grave decision that could affect it's whole life and that would also include the Spirits! It is then that the Spirit would use it's very positive influence to perhaps avert a tragedy that might come about if the physical was left to it's own devices!

Sometimes this influence goes unheeded and then it is left to the Spirit to try and restore a semblance of normality once again. But it always accepts that the physical body has the right to exert its freedom of will, just as it too has that gift of Free Will!!! And so there is what you might call a "clash of interests". But the Spirit knows that "it" is the one who is the visitor upon this planet and that Earth is the territory belonging to the physical body, so if mistakes are made by that one, they are if looked at in the right way, lessons to be learnt and overcome and in the doing so the Spirit can respond, for it too is learning. Though sometimes it feels that it's erstwhile companion of the Earth can sorely try it's, shall we say patience?!! But then that is what the Spirit has come to Earth to learn, patience and understanding! And those two lessons will stand it in good stead upon its true home upon the Spirit world!! So if "we" when we are that "human entity" can try and be more receptive to our Spirit companion, some might even call our Spirit our "conscience", what is in a name?!! If the outcome serves the right purpose then we can leave it at that!! Being human we have to live in a world that at times seems very difficult and not always fair but we should consider it a privilege to be part of the human race in spite of the ups and downs that seem to beset it!! But when we acknowledge that we do have a Spiritual side as well as a physical one and try and bring the two together then we will really start to live as we should. For what "we" as the human side of this joint venture upon life do, affects our Spirit side, and that is the "side" that goes on living long after the mortal body has ceased to exist, so what life has taught that body, the character that it has formed, how we feel towards each other, all these things the Spirit takes with it when it departs this Earth, so that mortal body has been a very, very necessary part of Spirits sojourn upon Earth and it never forgets what that body has contributed to it's learning and understanding, for each incarnated physical body will always remain a part of the Spirit that was it's life long companion, so though we as a physical body may only live for a certain time upon earth, we continue to live in the memory of our Spirit. Nothing is lost, it may alter, but is has meant something and that something means that our spirit has progressed, on its upward journey back home, which means God. So as a physical human being, we do matter and we are necessary and yes we are important in the scheme of things.

And if we can accept that and live not only a good physical life but one that incorporates our spiritual side as well, then our lives upon Earth have been worthwhile they are as God has intended them to be, a reflection of Him and His Love for us, both for our physical side and our Spirit side which one day will be united as the one and only, true Spirit, that part of God made manifest. We are Spirit for we come from Him and He is Spirit Personified. He lives in us, and we in turn, live because of Him, and through Him.

Learn to live and know your Spirit Self and let that side of you be your guiding light through life, so that others may feel that you have something that they want to share, and if you can share that, with love and compassion, then you are living the life that God wants you to.

That then is our lesson in life, to love one another and in doing so we are showing our Love for God, and so we leave you in that love and with the Blessing of that One on High. Peace be with you and also with you too little Scribe and fellow Brother in Christ. Farewell, Farewell.

Chapter 35

October 11th 2004 1.45 a.m.

SPACE! AN ENIGMA TO HUMANITY

This Earth that we think of as our "home", while "out there" we do not know if other Earth's exist and we think of them as "Alien", but are they? There is so much Life that abounds in the Universe, and we upon this planet have no real knowledge of it, We, that is this Earth planet are so small and yes insignificant if we did but know it. We look up to the Heavens and see stars, and certain planets that we have named, but as for knowing about what we think of as Space we are ignorant in the extreme for we see and yet we see nothing. And by nothing we mean the life force that does exist, even when we look and probe and find nothing and why? Because what is really Out There is NOT visible! The vibrationary force that permeates the whole of the Universe is so much higher and intense that we are virtually unaware of what is actually on our doorstep so to speak!!! As you travel further out into that Space, that is if you were able to, you would find that you would alter in your "physical construction" in fact you would cease to exist as a human being!!! Earthman has Not been programmed physically to be part of that vastness that seems to beckon him!! We upon the Earth can only exist upon this planet and we cannot exist beyond it!! Once this earth body of man has been shed and you call it "death", his true self which is made of entirely different material and you call it "Spirit", that is the essence that can exist in the invisible part's of the seen

Universe!! For there are vast area's that vibrate at such a high frequency that just cannot be observed by mortal man even with his antiquated telescopic lenses that he is so proud of!!! For they can only "see" or view, what he is capable of seeing with his "eyes". When if he were able to "see" not with his eyes but with the hidden senses of the Mind he would perceive wonders that would leave him gasping with disbelief!!!

This physical body that he uses upon Earth is of no use to him beyond that plane. The Spirit essence is what we are made of and that essence belongs to those area's that we have said are the invisibleness in space. They are the areas of reality and not those that are visible to man that he prides himself on being able to see!!

Your real Worlds are those of the Mind perception, not the Mind of the physical organ but the Mind of the Spirit quite a different matter altogether! As you are aware the Whole of the seen and the unseen Universe is one gigantic Electrical vibrationary force field, alive, in swirling masses of electrical discharges, it is the "stuff" that life is made of, the Spirit is the living part of this force, while Man upon the Earth plane is but a fraction of it, almost like the residue that is allowed to filter down to that lower sphere!

You upon Earth are affected in a minor way by these electrical discharges, and that is all, you have no idea of the true power of the life force that encircles your globe and keeps it in its orbital belt!! You are as it were protected from it's awesome power, because of your dense matter it cannot effect you to any great extent, but once released from that dense matter, for example at death, then the Spirit becomes fully aware of this force, it lives and breathes it, for it is now in it's true element!! It is now fully alive, vibrant and pulsating with energy. It is part of it's surrounding's, and is now capable of harnessing this force for it's own use, when it has been shown how to adapt to this life giving essence that it is a part of! Then those worlds that were invisible become visible as they have always been to those who are of the Spirit!!

Your Earth and those planets and stars etc that were your visible "play things" are now relegated to your present Spirit sense as "those invisible areas" that were once familiar to you, but no longer are!! Your heightened perceptions can now be released and you see life as it really is! Not static, but alive as never before!! You are now ready to experience what true life force can offer you, that is once your round of Earth incarnations have ceased for good!! That is now your past and can be forgotten, it has served it's purpose. And now your real life begins. Your character has been formed through those earthly experiences, you know now, who and what you really are, you are back upon the realms of the Spirit, no longer subject to the laws and restrictions of the lower spheres. Here you are "What you are". The hidden Worlds of the Spirit are now an open door for you to go through and explore. You have "grown up" as it were! And much is expected of you!!

And this is where we are told, we must leave you, for that time for you dear friends is not yet and will not be in the foreseeable future, but it will happen, believe that, when you are ready for it! And not before!!! Farewell! Farewell!

Little Brother Scribe we greet you, be patient for just a little while longer, all is well have no fear. We end this night's discourse with our Love for you all. Farewell.

Chapter 36

October 13th 2004

THOSE OTHER WORLDS AND THEIR INHABITANTS!

The World in which we live is one of many, and though not known to those who inhabit this planet, but nevertheless they do exist. They vary in what is known as density, and also their virbrationary force is far higher than this one that you know as your World! They are NOT what you may think of as planes of the Spirit. Their occupants are what you might term as "human beings". More or less the same as you but of a "lighter structure". By which we mean their "skeletal structure", their "bones" to be more precise! They are of a more pliable form, almost you might say "plastic". This gives them a greater freedom of movement in every way. Their bone structure is not prone to "breakage" or "fractures like those of the earth people.

They can "bend" their bodies in many ways that would no doubt astonish you if you were to see them. Their races are taller than yours with finer proportions, and their skin colouring is fairly uniform, though there are varying degrees, depending on where they live. Their bodies are not subject to deterioration in any way, no illness is found amongst the populations. Their intake of food is rather like your vegetarian's, they are not meat eaters and have never been. They respect the animal life and though there are a variety of what you would call "wild animals" these animals pose no threat to the human's, that is not to say that they can be made pets of, they remain in their allotted areas off habitation and do not venture beyond them. They too are vegetarians and killing for food is unknown to them. When the time comes for them to cease their life span, they go to an area of peace and quiet and just go to sleep, and as soon as the life force has left the body, it just disintegrates and returns to the earth from whence it was originated!!

Death as it is known upon Earth is quite different upon these other dimensions, when a human being (that is their variety of human beings) decides to leave their body and take up residence in their version of the Spirit world, that is exactly what they do, they (the Spirit) steps out of the physical body and by doing that the physical body just "vaporises", nothing left and the Spirit then transfers to the next plane of existence, usually remaining for awhile as a replica of its previous physical self of identification. Some will even continue as that identification indefinitely, for their Spirit and physical bodies are very close in their life cycles, and until they decide once more to reincarnate (if that is applicable to their evolutionary progress) they remain as they were, and even if they wish, continue the next incarnation as that same identifiable entity.

Their life spans are quite different to the Earth ones and can encompass sometimes several hundreds of years but their "years" are not the same as yours, which are lengthy, theirs are far less in times scale, much quicker and your one year would be equal to several of theirs, so its difficult to judge their true age for they have the ability to rejuvenate their skin and bodily tissue and muscles and all of their internal organs if they so wish!!! That is an option, but is not usually needed because their whole life style is one of health and vigour, they do not waste either their energy or their mental faculties, they adjust themselves to their surroundings and circumstances!! Difficult for you to understand but it is a normal procedure for them. They can quicken or slow down their metabolism as required, by thought manipulation. Like your Spirit planes, Thought is paramount and governs everything, in fact children are taught about the powers of thought almost from the cradle, it comes as second nature to them!!

Of course various Worlds or Planets do vary, but they are all of a much Higher form of life, than those of the Earth plane that is yours. And so it is reflected in their whole beings. They are gentler and kinder in every way, for they study each other and so there is no friction or forms of competitiveness, but do not think that that makes them weaker in any way! In fact that is their very strength. And when you upon your little Earth have learned that lesson then you will be welcomed by those others who you do not know about at present, but who can be thought of as your neighbours and your brothers!! But you have a long way to go before you can enjoy that integration with those from the outer spheres!!

It is possible for you, when you are upon the Spirit plane to shall we say, visit some of these other spheres, but only as a Spirit and not as a physical human being. You would be a "visitor a student" and you would be allowed to monitor their life styles for the purpose of furthering your evolution, you would only be "seen" by certain individuals who would have been previously contacted by your guides and teachers and they would be "your guides" upon their plane of habitation. So you would be able to "see" but not be "seen" by the majority of the population, but this education would be most beneficial to you, especially if you decided to reincarnate upon your own Planet Earth, you could then be teachers of those with whom you come into contact, you could enlighten them as to what you have learnt about those other planets and their inhabitants so that perhaps "in time" those upon your Earth would be in a better position when the time comes for the exploration of those as yet unknown and yes invisible to you, other worlds in the Universe!!

We feel that that is the right place for us to finish this discourse, it probably does not apply to you dear friends upon the earth but it perhaps has given you an idea of what does await you when the time comes!! We bid you an earnest Farewell.

Chapter 37

October 14th 2004 2.30 a.m.

PERCEPTIONS OF THE MIND

What do we really know about the World of the Spirit? Most people, and that is those who actually believe that there is a Spirit World think only in terms of the one that we all go to when the transition of the earthly body takes place. Well that is correct but there is more much more to it than just that! There are, shall we say, "degrees" upon the first plane of the Spirit world, so that some of us remain upon that "first degree" while others move swiftly through that phase and onto a "higher one" but it is till the first spirit plane!! It all depends on the growth of the spirit!! Which in laymans terms is, to what degree has the Spirit advanced during it's various "incarnations". For with each incarnation the Spirit has moved "upwards" in the cycle of it's evolutionary spiral!! So, for instance when the recently liberated spirit has gone "through" its assessment of it's recent past life upon Earth it may find that it is shall we say "entitled" to go straight through this first phase either onto the next one, or maybe even a higher one still!! It all depends on the degree of learning attained!!! Now when we say a "higher" degree that has been attained it is actually in the perception of the Spirits mental attitude and the "higher phase" that it goes to is in reality still a part of the first phase, but how can we put it? Think of when you were at school, and how as you progressed in your learning you went onto a "higher Class", still in the same school building, but now in a more advanced stage in the learning curve!! You were in a group of your "peers" and so you tended to associate with them at all times and that included the leisure time either at the school or afterwards! Do you follow what we are getting at?

You are still with the first group and yet you are not now "of it". Your life is progressing more rapidly than those you are leaving behind!! Just as you did while upon the Earth!! You are preparing yourself for the time when you leave school and "go out into the world" to earn a living!! Well here you are doing the same, but not to "earn a living" but to activate your latent possibilities, you now have a "purpose" in this ongoing life of yours. All sounds familiar doesn't it? Well it is, but on a "higher vibration". What you have learnt over these past incarnations fits you for your coming round of experiences that you will encounter now that you have awakened to your new responsibilities. For you do have them you know, you have progressed to this stage where you begin to see where you are going and how you are going to get there!! This world of the Spirit is a vast world of opportunities, and you are not "confined" to just one "area" so to speak, you graduate to where you are among those of a like mind, all progressing, all learning. The "spheres" we spoke of are those perceptions of the "mind" But they are still "realities". You are now ready to "go out into the World". Just as you did before, when you were in your physical body!! Your school learning was a preparation for your life to come, and the same applies here, Only on a "higher" sense, for you have earned that entitlement through your experiences of your past lives, with each physical incarnation and its subsequent further life upon the Spirit plane you are progressing, nothing is wasted, you recall and sift through the knowledge obtained and then move on!! Ever upward, even when it may seem to you a backward step if you have to venture into another physical incarnation, its all "progress" if you could but see it, which you do as you know, when another transition takes place!!! You may wonder sometimes if you are making any progress and the answer is Yes you are. It all takes "time" and let us face it, you really do have all the time in "the world", so do not despair, for each life brings you that much nearer to your ultimate goal of perfection and union with your Creator. There is a reason and there is a plan and you are part of it, so learn all you can about your lives to come so that you are prepared and can take advantage of what you have learned and so your advancement will be rapid because you deserve it!! Life really is very wonderful when you look at it properly and that means objectively and not with eyes closed but wide open, and we are not speaking of those of "sight" but the inner eyes of perception and understanding!! That are not eyes at all!!!

We feel that we will end our discourse and leave you to ponder upon what we have been discussing and see if it makes sense to you which we sincerely hope it does!!! And we say to you and the little scribe Farewell and may God's blessings be upon you. Farewell.

Chapter 38

October 16th 2004 3.00 a.m.

CAUSE AND EFFECT

Cause and Effect! In other words what people call "Karma" but what is it? And do we really understand what it means? People love to put things that they are not certain about into little pigeon holes, sometimes to forget them and at other times to think to themselves "I'll deal with that some other time" and then hopefully it may have sorted itself out!!! But supposing that with that word "Karma" and what it represent that we have got it all wrong?!! "It" is supposed to mean that if we have "wronged" someone in this Earthly life, somehow we have got to make recompense to them when we start our Spirit one after the transition of the body, But how can we do that, when as a Spirit and upon that plane, what could we do to overcome the hurt that was done on the physical? As a Spirit and for want of arguments sake, the one we hurt, is now also Spirit what can we do other than to say that we are genuinely sorry, we can't actually physically make amends, because it surely can't make any difference to one who is now a Spirit entity and would not need a physical act of remorse on our part that would result in the "debt" being paid!! Surely as Spirit's we would not require "recompense" in that way would we? We should be above all that, because understanding of past events upon the Earth plane would mean that is just what we would do. We would now understand and that includes both parties and so the only true act would be forgiveness and that should be an end of it!! That is if we have learnt anything during our lifetime regarding what life is all about and how we adapt to it!!!

I think perhaps that we put too much emphasis of this business of what we call "Karma". Quite often I feel, we do pay this thing called debt, while we are still alive, in one way or another, and if we have truly learnt our lessons when upon the Earth, then this act of contrition should not be required when we are back in the realms of the Spirit should it?

Now I am not talking about acts of violence that may have been done upon Earth. That I'm sure would require a completely different form of forgiveness and understanding, but there again as "Spirits" we would see things as they not only were but are, and that would mean that lessons if that is the appropriate word to use, have been learned and are being learnt here and now, all part of the ongoing life cycle that we are all a part of!!!

It certainly must require great strength of character to not only say "I forgive you" but also for the other one to say "I am truly sorry". Isn't that what life is supposed to be about? We are our own Judge and Jury and therefore we would or should know how to handle these situations! I realize that I have only touched the surface of this situation and that there must be deeper areas that require deeper solutions to them, but then surely that is why we are upon the Earth plane in the first place, to learn, to overcome, to try and understand, and above all to forgive. Easier said than done, but then that is "Life" isn't it? Perhaps we look at things the wrong way round and make perhaps mountains out of molehills. Though I'm sure some people will say "He doesn't know what he's talking about, you can see he hasn't lived, otherwise he wouldn't say what he does"!!! Perhaps they are right, who knows? I can only say what I feel about things and I don't know whether I'm right or wrong!!! But surely when we are all Spirits upon the Spirit plane, things that happened to us on the Earth plane will be seen in a completely different way, now that we can view them from a distance so to speak!! In other words, we understand the reason "Why" and because of that our perception of things may be completely altered!! Karma either good or bad should be worked out while we are still upon the Earth plane and should not be "carried over" either to the Spirit world of left until another incarnation take's place, which is then really the responsibility of the incarnating Spirit and not the fault of the human entity that it is using. And this I feel is where most people are in error, for that Karma good or bad can not be attributed to them, that is the one that is now being used by the Spirit. It would not be justice to lumber them with what really was nothing to do with them, for the present physical vehicle was not the one who lived in that previous incarnation it was and is the Spirit who is the continual link in both lives and existences and so it is to that one that all of this applies. That is why I feel we aught to look at "Karma" in a different light than what we have been either brought up to understand or how we think of it!!!

Justice! That is what it should be about and not a form of "compensation" that we feel is our due!!! And the only way we are going to overcome what I feel is an error of judgement is by Love in its truest sense. Universal Love that overcomes all obstacles and frees the Soul from the bondage of the continual reincarnation upon the plane of Earth and allows it to proceed upon its upward journey back to the God head and unity with the Creators. And that is where I think I will finish. And say to you God Bless you and keep you safe.

Reading that over I feel I have ended rather abruptly, but I do feel I have come to the end of what I have been talking about though I'm sure there is a lot more explaining that could be done, but I don't think I'm in a position to do it, so this is where I really will end my discourse and hope that you the reader or listener as the case may be will think about what has been said and then make up your own mind as to whether you feel there may be some truth in what I've been trying to say!! And so I'll say Farewell like my Brothers do! Farewell and God bless you.

"The Little Scribe".

Chapter 39

October 19th 2004 1.35 a.m.

WORDS FAIL ME!!

We pose you a question Brother, or shall we say a conundrum? Are we Physical? Are we Spirit? Or are we more than that one that we think of as the Real and only true one that we posses?!! Could it be that we, that is you and I, in fact all of us, are even more, much more than what we are told we are?!! Is there somewhere upon a distant sphere, not even seen or as yet known about, a dwelling place of habitation far beyond our present understanding, where these other variations of what can be termed "ME" exist? Are we "multiple"? Not just one, or two or even three, but even more, what might be called "Bodies" or "Personalities" that go beyond what is considered our Normal Self, which has always been thought of as "Spirit"?!! Are these "abstract personalities" another "life form"? Unheard of and beyond our present comprehension?

Can it be that we do not as yet know just "Who" we really are? Is there somewhere beyond our present reach an "Essence" that houses what we cannot envisage, that has no name that can explain what that essence incorporates?!!! Let us think for awhile, and when I say Think I mean retreat within one's mind self go into the blackness of nothingness and past experience, and "See" what that blackness can reveal to that inner "sight", or should I say "Perception"?!!!

Can you envisage what "that" could be?!!! Or is it beyond your present human mind understanding? For Mind is Pure Thought in its original conception and there again What constitutes "Thought"? How can one perceive what one cannot "see", "touch", or understand, what "thought" consist of?!!! Is Thought that "Essence" that I have spoken of? Or is it "within" that essence? Is it "part of it" or does "Thought" clothe the unknowable??!! Just who and what are we really? Would that word "Spirit" be sufficient to enlighten us on that subject? Though haven't I said in the beginning of this discussion that we are even beyond that term that we use called Spirit? I feel that our or rather your present brain capacity is not capable of translating thought into a positive perception of what I am speaking to you about!! Is there anyway with your limited knowledge and intelligence that I can explain in your form of language what I am trying to convey to you?! What analogy can I conjure up that could allow you to say "Ah!" I can see what "He" means?! A "Vapour" not one that is "Porous" and translucent, but a vapour that is "solid" and yet at the same time does not exactly "exist" for it cannot be "seen" with the outer sight of a human body!! Yet it is there, and can materialize if that word gives you some idea of "its" "possibilities" as "anything" that a thought can conjure up, and that "anything" can be beyond the original "thought" it can be? Shall I say a spirit essence? A physical body of reference? One of the many facets of the You that you can identify as You and no one else? Yet that "Vapour like substance" could be everywhere, you could be part of it and yet separate from it and still be part of it!!! Can you follow just a little of what I am trying to explain to you? You that is not just the identifiable you as a person the word "You" signifies All of mankind in this instance. You are part of and yes from the Primordial Essence of Pure Thoughts! Life! Before it becomes life as you think you understand what that word means!! Can you grasp the meaning that I am trying to convey to you little Brother of the Night? Think! Think! Think! And you will know who you are part of!! Yes! You little person, All of the forms of life, and the word I do not divulge, for it is the word above all others and is Sacred. For that is what you are part of!!

You have been given knowledge this night that you must think about in the quietness of your mind and come to your own conclusion. You do not know Me though "I" am fully aware of who you are and have been, and are to be!!!! I have spoken in the Singular this night and not in your usual acceptance of "We"! For I an Not of that band of travelling Brothers in White though it is through their generosity that I have been allowed to use your "vehicles" of Mind transportation, for which I am truly grateful. Yes in answer to your thought little being of light, We shall meet one day but not for some while, though I shall contact you again, for you now belong to my Aura and so you are in essence a part of Me!! As I am of you!!

It is time for Me to withdraw from this discussion and so I am informed that when I leave you I should say Farewell which in your language does Not mean Goodbye but just a parting of the thought power. And so I bid you little Brother of the Night time Farewell my Soul companion Farewell.

Brother! We also say Farewell and this Nights discourse has been one of great privilege for you little friend, believe that. Farewell.

Chapter 40

October 22nd 2004

WHEN PERFECTION IS REACHED

Further to my thoughts regarding our "Spirit selves". When you look upon the Religious painting of the past, the Holy Spirit is usually depicted as a "white dove". So it would seem that artists in those days really didn't know what the "Spirit" looked like and so they thought a "white dove" seemed the most appropriate way of what they were trying to express but what they actually didn't know in reality! And so down the ages, Spirit, and that goes for all of us for the sake of argument, and so Spirit has become identified with the human body that is its temporary "home" during its incarnation period! And if you were to ask most people how they would describe their Spirit if they could see it, they would probably say "Well it looks like me doesn't it?" and of course we do have statements from Doctors and Nurses that are attending a dying person and those with a clairvoyant nature even if they do not think of it in that light. They Say, they have seen the Spirit leave the body at death and it looks just like the body that is resting upon the hospital bed! And they would be quite right, for the Spirit has the ability so to speak, of being able to "assume" whatever likeness it wishes, depending upon the situation! But actually the Spirit in, its shall we say "Normal state" does not resemble an Earth like body, it is made up of "essences" from the original Creator, the one most people think of as their God! When upon the first Spirit plane that is part of the Earth one, the Spirit is usually observed as the likeness of the human body that it inhabited upon Earth, mainly because of family ties linking the various members of the Earth family, and those that have departed the Earth retain that likeness for obvious reasons. But when the Spirit advances to the next plane of habitation it resumes it natural and normal mode of identification. For on that plane a human like body is not required for its advancement. Though many do still prefer to take on the appearance of a human body, even if it does not resemble its previous Earthly one!!!

Like wise even upon the first Spirit plane that we spoke of the Spirit can revert to its "original form" if it so wishes if the situation requires it!!! This is its own Spirit essence, not the physical identifiable body that it has been in the habit of using!! For in some "areas" of that first plane there are advanced schools of learning where the Spirit is shown some of its latent possibilities regarding the ability to "thought manipulate" and that covers a vast amount of "data" that the Spirit is heir to!!!

Spirit in its "normal state" is a form of Oval shaped iridescent light emanation which is vibrant and alive with energy, It "gives off" electrical impulses in varying degrees of colour formation, while at the same time it "houses" at its central core the mind essence which can resemble a "spirit entity" of great beauty. This "essence" can assume proportions that can be gigantic according to human understanding, or on the other hand it can reduce its size to almost what you might term the head of a pin!!! This then is the Mind essence that the Soul is created of which in turn has the ability to create anything that it needs to further its knowledge and understanding of what it is a "part" of, and this is, as you are aware the whole reason for its creating "Spirit essences" that dwell upon the various planes leading downwards to the Earth plane and are the same planes that the Spirit uses upon its upward journey back to its creative source!!

The circle metaphorically speaking in complete!! The Life cycle that encompasses the Soul and its various entities we call the Spirit when completed to the Creator's satisfaction becomes once more part of that Creative essence and now begins its second stage where it is part of the ongoing creative process, it can in time if it wishes become what you would term a "Creator in its own right"! But! This ability is given to only a few and even then only after a lengthy period of "probation". But the reward of being part of this "band of Creators" and knowing that you are one with them is the highest accolade that you can aspire to.

That then is the "Perfection" that we have sought for all through our various lives and incarnations. We actually have spoken of the "exceptions", regarding the creative process. Most of us will reach a form of Perfection that is possible for us to achieve and enjoy, so take heart little denizens upon the Earth plane, set your sights upon a goal that you can reach and not one that is an impossibility for most of mankind!!!

We bid you Farewell and wish you well in your coming lifespan not only upon earth but upon the many spheres that await you.

Farewell little Brother! We seem to take over from you, when you have started your writing, but that is as it is intended and we thank you little friend we truly do.

Farewell from all of Us, your Brothers of Light. Farewell.

Chapter 41

October 25th 2004 2.00 a.m.

TRUTH AND ITS CONSEQUENCES!

Cast your mind back to when you were in your early twenties and you asked "What is the Truth" and the answer you received via your thoughts was "Know the Truth and the Truth will make you free". At that time though you accepted what you had been told, it lay dormant in your subconscious until later, quite a few years later I believe, but you did remember and it started you on your road of discovery, of which you are still on!!! Quite an achievement is it not when all that you asked for was "The Truth"!!! Just like the saying From little acorns grows the mighty Oak tree!! No little friend you are not yet a mighty oak tree, but you are well on the way to becoming one!!! That should give you food for thought!! But do NOT get carried away with that metaphor, for you are but one of many if the truth is known, but you do belong to a band of dedicated beings of light that you are aware of!! So you see little brother from just a question that at the time was just a question the answer to it has now at this present time born fruit. One can never tell, that is the human side of ones character, what one has shown an interest in what one might call the inner life of the physical body!!!

All over your Planet there are souls that are being awakened in the Spiritual sense, for this is a time when your Planet is being tested, and that includes those who also inhabit it!! You are witness at this time to what you can call "Global Disruption". Your Scientists and those who are the Thinkers of your world call it "Global Warming", the "Greenhouse Syndrome" they give it various names but never the correct one! Which is "The Spiritual Awakening" of those with ears to hear and eyes to see with!! And we are not speaking of those organs of the physical body that you use daily!!!

There is an upsurge of Psychic Intuition that is being beamed down to your World from the Spirit Realms in an attempt to make Man aware of his inner abilities, those of the Mind and the Spirit, for it is those two qualities that he has so far neglected in his search for what he thinks is his rightful place of happiness in this world, that is being torn apart, because of Man's short sightedness and his own selfish desires for the playthings of the mortal body!!! Greed! Is what we are talking about, Greed in its ugliest sense, for Greed is a selfish motive and never incorporates the feelings of others, but Greed is an ugly sore that festers and only brings forth more unsightly sores, and War is but one of them!!!

Your present "leaders" are if you did but realize it, are leading you to oblivion, oblivion of the Spirit as well as of the Body of Flesh"" Wake up"" Turn your thoughts back to when you believed in a God, He is still there, in spite of the way Man tries to ignore his very presence in everything that is good around him!! You are all Brothers regardless of the colour of your skin or the trapping of your so called Religious cultures, which do not seem to us to have any kind of relationship to the One on High that your Religions pretend to adhere to! They pay lip service which is hollow, while they seek to exploit those weaker Nations who have for too long been deprived of the very wealth that is under their feet, there again Greed rears its ugly head and all the sensibilities of others needs are wilfully neglected, and all under the guise of progress. And progress for whom? Not the downtrodden for sure!! Your World is like a bubbling cauldron of Hate that is gradually destroying the very fabric of your Earth, you cannot go on destroying it the way you are, your food chain is on the brink of disintegration you substitute what the Earth can provide with synthetic food stuffs that lack the nutriments that is for the sustaining of life, not just for the body but the Spirit as well!!

What you put into your body should in theory be nourishment for Body and Spirit. Think about that! For one without the other will cease to exist!! The body may well remain but without its Spirit to guide it, it is a hollow shell. Think about that and know that we speak the Truth. Don't ignore what inside you is trying to tell you. Live for one another and not off one another! There is still enough for all of your needs both physical and Spiritual, give when those in need ask for it! Don't make them beg. This World can be a wonderful place to live upon if only you learn to co-operate with each other, look beneath the outer covering of skin and you will find that basically you are all the same. You are all the Children of the ONE GOD, respect the differences in each other, nourish them, for that is what makes life worth while. That is why you are upon this Earth of yours, to show you that you can live in harmony if you try, for it is the only way to really Live! For if you do not heed the advice given then surely you will reap the whirlwind of destruction, you and your Earth will have to be "cleansed" and we dare not tell you of what that would mean!!

We leave you on that note of gloom! Change yourselves before it is too late for if you don't it will be done for You and you will have no choice in the matter. Think! Think! Think! And then act accordingly. We bid you a sad Farewell!! You little scribe need not fear we watch over you. Farewell.

Chapter 42

October 28th 2004 12.05 a.m.

THE CHANGING WORLD

When you think of the Universe what is it that comes to your mind? The Vastness? The bewildering array of Stars? The Constellations? The Planets? The choice is never ending!! But do you think that you have seen all that there is to be seen? Or do you perhaps wonder if what you can perceive is but a fraction of what really lies out there and yes even beyond what you call the perimeter of your known universe!! You "see" with your physical eyes aided by those enormous telescopic lenses that seem to bring some of those heavenly bodies just a little closer and yet they remain so very far away, and what can you do about it?!! Your scientific bodies have their theories, and that is all, they try to work things out, and let us be fair they have succeeded in finding our just a little of what is really "out there", but there is so much more, much, much, more! That if you could see what is there you would be astonished and realize how little you actually do know, and even that little is constantly changing, so that what is observed today is gone tomorrow figuratively speaking!! You cannot take anything in Space for granted. What is seen hides what you cannot see!! And here we speak of the unseen planets and spheres that to you are invisible but who actually do exist!! And not just in someone's fertile imagination!!

"Space" if you could really become part of it would not only amaze you, but you would have to exist in another dimension to really observe what to you now would just be an emptiness with just a collection of planet's that you have given names to, in the hope of identifying some form of "Life force" upon them similar to your own!!!

It is Out there but you upon the Planet Earth are not yet ready to become part of that "Life Force" which has been in existence long, long, before your little world came into being! And will still be there if and when this World of yours has ceased to exist!! As it will in time!! You are meant to be custodians of this planet, looking after it for those who are to follow you, but you are not making a very satisfactory job of it are you? What with your War's and your wanton destruction of the very life force of this little Earth!! It has become something of an unstable place, but one in which human beings can live in harmony with what you term Nature if they try. For Nature as you call it, is a Force that is so powerful that to you could be called unbelievable!! The inner core of this planet of yours is very active at present and it must be allowed to expend its energy in the only way it can, with earthquakes, typhoons, tornadoes, and volcanic eruptions!! You have to accept all of these disturbances for they are necessary if your world is to continue to be of use in the evolutionary sense!!!

Your world is gradually becoming not exactly smaller, but more compact as it was in the beginning of your cycle of Birth, Life, and Death!!! You cannot stop what has begun, but you can adapt to the change if you wish to survive as a human race upon a dense human environment you know as Earth!!

There have been many such Earths as yours, some have ceased to exist and have become part of other worlds or planets! Others have "gone on" to become "Higher realms", those that are part of the Invisible source that we hinted at. Nothing is lost or wasted, it just alters, for life once created does not die as you think of dying, it changes yes, it alters yes, but is still remains a "life force". That is the living part of what is known as the Creator, though that word hardly describes what that Creative Principle is! For "It" is beyond any description that any form of language could seek to identify with!! You have your Aspects of that Force and you know them as God or Gods if you wish. For they are Your Creators, just accept that term for them and seek no further to extend your knowledge, for it is forbidden at the present, for Man as you know him is not capable mentally to accept what is True but cannot be verified as the Truth, for the Truth would throw him into a turmoil and his mind would explode with the unleashed knowledge!!! Do not go beyond the outer area's of your mind, you can only guess at what is true with your inner senses, and even then you have no yardstick with which to judge what is and what is not! Leave well alone until you are once more upon the Universal plane of the Spirit, where truth can be seen for what it is!!! Think about it, but do not delve any deeper for your own peace of mind!!!

Remember the Invisible Realms of habitation that we spoke of? Some of those Realms could be what you upon Earth call your "Spirit Worlds"!!! Invisible, but never the less realities, that you do know of but do not always remember. We speak here of the majority of humanity and not those who could be identified as the Silent Minority that will one day be recognized for who and what they are, for they are the Teachers, not in the accepted sense but never the less that is what they are! And they will be the Salvation of Mankind, if Mankind will only listen to them with an open mind and a heart full of Love. And here we feel is where we will leave you after this nights discourse. Do not be disheartened by what we have said. This will not apply to many of you upon the Earth at this time, but it is a warning to those who will follow you and that is all that we are allowed to say on this subject. We leave you with God's Blessing's and His Love and little Brother Scribe, you know what we wish you, for you are indeed a brother of light one of us! We bid you Farewell little friend as we do to all of those of you upon the Earth plane! Farewell.

Chapter 43

October 29th 2004 1.35 a.m.

THE MEANING OF LIFE

Is there an answer to the question What is Life and why are we living it? Some people will immediately say there is No reason, we are born, we live and then we die and that's that!! Why try and delude yourself that there must be a reason!! There isn't one and that's final!!!

Well dear friends that answer I'm afraid is not as isolated as you may think. Many people especially in this present time upon Earth feel that there seems to be no rhyme or reason for living, but these IS! And there always has been, and always will be. We understand when people feel like that, for in spite of all the material advantages that today's population have, they feel that there is an emptiness to their lives, they just cannot see a purpose however small it may be! And why should this negative attitude be so prevalent today, in spite of what we have said regarding all the material advantages that people seem to have!!! and you notice we have used the phrase "seem to have" now that would imply that those so called "advantages" do not satisfy those people and they are looking for an alternative that will give them an answer that will satisfy this longing! Is there an Answer?!! We say to you "Yes! There is" and it is a very simple one! It is, bring back God and what He stands for into your every day existence and when you do, you will find that a purpose, is shown to you, you can cease your searching for the answer that you have sought lies within you all the time! It starts with the words "Love one another". When you can honestly say that you not only do, but you put into practice what these words mean, then that word "purpose" has been answered loud and clear!!

We must not look for an answer upon the physical plane of life, but upon the one we call "Spiritual". A word that we are afraid does not mean to today's population's what it once did, even just a decade or so ago!! The youth of today have grown up too fast but they lack the experience of living. The older generation may have had harder life styles, but somehow it made them better people, they cared more for each other and for the simple things of life. They didn't crave for things that they knew were out of their reach! In other words they were more satisfied with what they had. But today, the idea of what it is that you posses of the material variety will give you the satisfaction that you feel is lacking in your life is proving to be hollow.

Look around you, that is you people of the Western hemisphere, and what do you see? Pictures in your papers and; upon your television screens that say "you must have this" if you want a life style that you feel you need! "You Need!!" Now that is a hollow situation to be sure! You do not need a fraction of what you are told you should have for a happy life. Your present day Society is one of what you have today is forgotten tomorrow, while you search for something to replace what it is that you feel you are lacking! And what you are lacking is Love and compassion for one another. Deep down we have a tribal instinct we belong to groups of like minded people, that is what the word society means. A Social Life not one in isolation either of the body or the Spirit!! We all need each other if we are to grow in stature and yes character!! It is how you get on with your neighbour and we are not talking about the person "next door", though today "they" certainly are important if you wish to live in harmony!! But neighbour can mean those people who live on the other side of your World, the Developing Countries, and just what are you in the West doing to help them in this development? For far to long you have been "holding them back" afraid that if they are given the freedom that is rightfully theirs, they may one day "overtake you". So you give with one hand and take it back with the other!! You are "Hypocrites" and you know it!!! There is enough for everyone if only you learn to share in the distribution of it, and that not only means food, but with the tools for them to be independent and yet still part of the World's diverse populations. Not strangers, and that you call foreigners, but Brothers in the broadest sense. We all have something to give to each other that will make a difference to their lives and that something is Love, Universal love that gives without expecting something in return, and yet when you give that Love freely, you do get something in return, its called the satisfaction of knowing that you are trying to live a life that is a good life a God life. It really is as simple as that. Don't go on isolating yourselves, for your World is getting smaller by the minute and what affects you here, has its repercussions across the water's tomorrow!!

That then is the reason for living that you have been searching for, its living with and for each other. Forget your differences and build upon the things that can bind you together, so making this World in which you all live a happier and safer place for your future generations to thrive in, in peace and that means in prosperity as well!! The effort required is not a difficult one it may mean sacrificing some of the things that you thought were important to you, and once you have forgotten them you'll find that you'll feel better for it!! So go forward, you do have a purpose in life and the purpose is to live as good a life as you are able to, do your best, and that is what life is all about!!

We leave you upon that note of hope and ask for the Blessings of the One on High to be with and upon you now and forever, and so we bid you Farewell.

And to you little Brother Goodnight and God bless you. Peace be with you, Farewell.

Chapter 44

October 31st 2004 12.15 a.m.

WE ARE ONE YET WE ARE MANY!

We bring you Peace dear Brother. We bring you Peace. How shall we begin? So much has been written over the ages regarding Man and his destiny, his destiny of Life. And just what is this destiny? Is it that he is to find his way back to his very roots, or is there something else that he has to find? You may say "Well if there is what is it?" "Surely finding his way back to his root source is his primary objective in life?" is it Not?!!! The answer to that is "Yes", but on the way there he has to find something else, and that "something" is Himself! For when he does then he really will be back to his roots!!! For his "roots" lie within him all the time and he knows it not!!

And here we pause, for Man is more than just this physical body that he inhabits while upon the Earth plane!! We tell you that that body is but a cloak, a cloak that covers the true identity of who it is that dwells within!! You call that one "your Spirit". But even then you are more than that, for the Spirit is yet another cloak for Him to put on, in this journey back and forth in his quest for his true identity!! Man and we will still call him that, has many identities, during this journey of the Soul!! And why you may ask should he need these various identities that are loosely called bodies? For "body" is a term associated with the Physical person, and yet that word body is also used to illustrate these other forms that are also His!! "Light" is one of them, "Higher" is another and yes there are others also including the word "Essence" a word that means so much and yet is not really understood! For essence is another word for that part of Man that is Divine!

This physical part of Man is shall we say the most misunderstood garment that he has to put on while upon the lower plane of Earth!! "It" is but a "cloak", and not as important as he thinks it is! For it is the one that he most frequently "casts aside" as it ages and eventually dies!! While all of his other cloaks of identity are changed but do not die in the sense that the physical one does!! His true self which incidentally is more than just "Self", for "self" means very little when you compare it to the Whole! Of which we, that is Man is but a part of!! For the Whole cannot be identified to Man's complete satisfaction!! That! Will be shown Him later, when He understands who He really is, or perhaps we should say who he thinks he is!!!

All very bewildering you may think, all of this Who he thinks he is, and Essence, and Light and Higher! And even more!!! We will speak of the One that is shall we say the original go between that connects all these various aspects that go to make up Man in his "entirety"!! Spirit is the one aspect that Man upon the earth plane accepts as his other self. If you tell him of these other aspects that are "Him", he will either not believe you or say "Why do I need these other so called "aspects", what are they for, and where are they? tell me that"!!! and so for the present we will concentrate on the one called "Spirit"!! This particular "aspect" is the nearest to what we can call the "Human body". It is the one that "dwells" within that body for the lifetime that that body exists. And yet the word "Dwells" is not quite accurate, for the true essence of the Spirit, dwells upon the Spirit plane, and what is commonly thought of as the one that dwells within Man, is an aspect of that Spirit!! Confusing?!! Yes, to you it is, but in reality it is not!!!

What you think of as your Spirit is your own Higher sense that you bring with you when you, as a human being are brought into existence. That Higher sense goes with you wherever you as Spirit go!!! It is the Christ Spirit that man was given when The Christ

Spirit of Jesus the Teacher of Righteousness left the body of that one and returned to the Creator that you know of as God! And as He promised He left within all of Mankind that part known as the Christ Spirit, that Divine Essence that cannot be seen but only felt!! Many people will call it their conscience! Of what is right or wrong the name means nothing, it is the results that count. That then is the part that our Spirit taps into from time to time, it, shall we say, is the "Overseer" of the physical vehicle that is its counterpart upon earth!! It takes into account all that the physical vehicle is capable of during its life time and retains all that it considers is relevant in its upward journey in the cycle of evolution, its evolution Not the physical bodies, which has served its purpose, its part that is necessary to the Spirits understanding of who it is! And this dear friends takes in many lifetimes before it can dispense with this cycle of re-incarnation upon the Earth plane! And can then proceed upon its journey that really begins once these re-incarnation periods have ceased!!!

They are a necessary part of the Spirit's "education", but they are only a part, there are many more shall we say incarnations of those various aspects that we spoke of earlier! And with each one so we draw ever nearer to the completion of our task that was set us, when we were created from that Divine source that we are but a part of!! And to understand what that truly means to us, who are the very thoughts of the Creator, in manifested form, to the goal that we are programmed to reach, and we add, eventually! The journey is long, as long as time itself, but as you are well aware Time is not what it seems to be, for Time is just another form of creation of the Creator and does not necessarily mean the same upon other spheres that we gravitate to!!! And so if you care to think and think carefully you may come to the conclusion that time as you think you know it does not really exist at all!! Like all of Life and that means all lives Illusion plays a prominent part, for Illusion and Reality are both sides of the One coin, and that coin IS? Have you guessed what it is? Then we have no need to tell you have we?!!

We feel that here is a good a place as any to end this nights discussion, for if we were to pursue this subject further, just where would it get you?! You are not yet ready to accept what we could impart to you and it would no doubt confuse you even further!!! And so we will bid you our customary Farewell and may you receive the Blessings from the Ones on High, Farewell dear Earth friends Farewell.

And to you little Brother Scribe we send you our Love and our Blessings and we say to you ALL is WELL, believe that for it is the Truth.

Farewell little friend Farewell. And do not be too hard on yourself for you are only human aren't you? Farewell.

Chapter 45

November 2nd 2004

EVERY CLOUD HAS A SILVER LINING!

Sometimes when you are sitting quietly, perhaps in the glow of the firelight and you let your mind wander back to the days of your youth, memories of happiness, memories that you treasure when the world seemed like your oyster that contained a pearl of great price, and that pearl was the life ahead of you, where all things were possible, only now when you look back upon it, has it turned out how you hoped it would, those ambitious plans that you had in your head, did they mature? Or did the journey of life take you down another path and those plans never quite materialised as you thought they should have?

We all have dreams when we are young, but sadly to most people that is all they are, just dreams!! But wait! Think about it, you are now what life has made you, and really it hasn't been too bad has it? You've had many disappointments, but then again you've had times when everything went well and the disappointments turned out to be but stepping stones along life's pathway, they proved to be beneficial in the long run for in overcoming them and seeing them for what they were, made you a stronger person, and the next so called disappointment, you overcame remarkably easily , you had learnt a valuable lesson, not to give in to despair, but to look for a solution to any problem you had to face. That is what life is all about isn't it? It's not straight forward, you don't know just what it is that is waiting for you round the corner!! But as you grow in stature you likewise grow in character, and that is something that no one can take away from you, it is yours, you've earned it and its yours to keep and take with you wherever you may go, and that doesn't only mean upon this Earth plane of yours!!

We build upon our character each day, it is what sustains us through life's vicissitudes, even when perhaps we feel that life hasn't always seemed fair to us! But just like the old saying "Every cloud has a Silver lining". That is if you look for it, and it doesn't always show itself to you straight away. You have to find it for yourself, but it is there waiting to be uncovered, and when it is! Well then you can go forward once more!! We come to Earth to learn about ourselves, that is our real selves, Our Spirit knows what it is that it lacks but it takes a lifetime upon Earth in fact quite often many lifetimes before it reaches the point when it no longer has to take upon itself a physical body to show it what it is searching for! The Earth plane is a good training ground for the Spirit, for it has to contend with situations that are only found upon the Earth and yet they have a bearing upon the next sphere that the Spirit really belongs to. Overcoming those situations are what the physical and the Spiritual bodies of integration are all about. One needs the other, even if at a certain time they have to part company and one gets left behind! But the memory of that one goes with the Spirit for ever, nothing gets lost, believe that for it is true! It is all those physical journeys that the Spirit takes that makes it what it is and enables it to progress in its own world of habitation. These earth lives are very important and necessary not only to the Spirit but to the physical body that it is loaned for that brief span upon Earth.

As a physical human being we sometimes wonder just what all this life is about, we don't always think that we need our Spirit as much as it needs us!!! It's the blending of those two aspects, the seen and the unseen that forms the character of this joint venture of the two that are really ONE, and that ONE is the manifested part of the Creator God, that will one day return to its Creator, knowing who it really is, and ready to be what all of this training has been for, to be a Co-Worker with the Almighty, to do what it is that is required of us wherever that may be. This then will be the start of our Real life of Service, one that we have become fitted for, we can in our own way show to our Creator that we return His Love of Us, by sharing that Love with those who are in need of it, Wherever they may be! And think not only of the plane of Earth, for there are many such spheres in our vast Universe that can respond to Love, that is Universal Love that knows no bounds, and is free to all who need it!! That then is the goal to which we have been striving to reach even when we were not aware of it. Life has a purpose and you are that purpose, believe that and go forward together in partnership. Body and Spirit, Spirit and Body, that part of the Almighty made visible to one and all!!

We bid you Farewell dear friends we bid you Farewell!

May Allah be praised!!!

Chapter 46

November 3rd 2004 12.30 a.m.

RELEASE THE SPIRIT WITHIN

We greet you little Brother and we say to you "God bless you and keep you safe.!

We begin tonight's discourse with the words "KNOW THYSELF"! Very few of us can actually say that we truly know ourselves, that is know ourselves who we really are. And just who it that?!! We see our reflection in a mirror and we think I know you! But do we? The reflection that stares back at us is not who we really are, for that reflection is of the physical body that we, the Spirit are temporarily inhabiting! Look beneath the surface of that face that you behold and try and see who it is that lies hidden there!! Difficult is it not? For our true self, our Spirit self cannot be seen with our physical eyes, you have to look deeper, beyond the reflection of those eyes that seem to be asking a question, look just a little longer, and then close those eyes of the mortal body, and the see if you can behold the one who is really there all the time. But you must surrender all outward thoughts and seek the inner senses of the mind. See not with sight but with feeling! And if you are truly searching for the one who you really are you will discover what is there, but which is not visible to that one whose reflection you have seen in the mirror! Just stay awhile in that quiet reverie, and when you once more open the eyes of the physical body you will know that you have been in contact with that other you and the feeling that you feel will be one of deep, deep gratitude for you have, for just a brief spell been in communion not just with your own Spirit, but with the Spirit Essence of the One that must remain nameless, but who never the less is who you really are, for ;you are part of that Divine substance that brought you into existence in a time that you no longer remember and yet the feeling of belonging is so strong that you can almost feel the tie of that kinship that is beyond description of the physical body that you now inhabit, but which is a "reality" in every sense of the word. These feelings however brief are ones that will last, for your Spirit has made itself known to you and you will never feel quite the same again, for you now know that you are more than that reflection of your physical cloak of identification. You are a part of that Creative Principle that you know as the "Godhead"! Hence forth live and act in that knowledge. Let that part of you take charge of your daily life, you are now firmly on the path back to the source from which you originated no longer just a physical body but one of the Spirit that knows itself as such! You are Alive not only from without but from Within and with this realization those with whom you come into contact will benefit from your inner knowledge even if they do not quite understand what it is that you are imparting to them, they will feel the effect, and their lives will be the better for the influence that you, with your inner Spiritual awareness are giving to them, you have become a channel for Gods Love to flow through you and into them and by this act of love, they in their turn will also become a channel, even if they do not know it. For God's Love breaks down all known barriers and makes of a stranger a friend and that is God's Law working through each and every one who has a heart that is open and full of Love for his fellow man!!

When Man releases this love within him instead of hiding it from view then you really will find that this life upon Earth is worth living, and Heaven is within the grasp of all, for Heaven is not a place but a genuine feeling of Love for one another and so Heaven can become a reality while you still dwell upon this lower plane of Earth. This then is your lesson for tonight's discussion, release the Spirit within, listen to that inner voice and act upon it, do not push it aside to think about it another day, for another day is today!!! And today will soon become yesterday, think about that, and don't let life slip past you without you realizing it. For a day that is past cannot be reclaimed, it has gone forever!! Make each day a lifetime of endeavour for this lifetime is but one of many that await you, when you learn that this physical one is the prelude to the one that is everlasting the one that you call Spirit.

And so we will leave you on that note. We bid you Farewell and leave you in God's care.

Little Scribe, Farewell dear friend Farewell, God bless you!

Chapter 47

November 7th 2004 1.00 a.m.

MIND AND HOW TO USE IT

Open up your Mind to the wonders that await you upon your final transition to the Realm of the Spirit! Your true home the one that you had to leave to gain the knowledge of who you really are! And who is that? Have you discovered your true identity yet? Or are you somewhat hampered in that discovery, by the mortal body of flesh that you at present inhabit? You little Brother are Not unique for this awakening occurs to all who are the seekers of the truth!! And they are not confined to what is called the intelligentsia! In fact what is termed as one of high intelligence can often be a stumbling block, for the Mind can be at times a fickle Master if it is not properly controlled by what we like to call our Spirit!

The Mind must be a servant to the Spirit and not its Master!! Though it will try to be if you are not careful! For the mind is full of tricks perhaps not always intentionally, but it is a very powerful tool that you have to learn how to use and more importantly how to control!!

You may think that seems rather strange when the Mind is such an important part of our complete "make up". But like all parts of the "body" and here we are speaking not only of the Spirit, but for the time being the Physical dwelling place of the Spirit while it tarries upon the Earth plane!! The Mind is the active part of Both bodies and all at the same time, even though they both differ in shall we say structure. For the physical body is of a somewhat gross material, and do not misunderstand that word gross it just denotes the bodily make up that is needed while dwelling upon the Earth of dense matter as opposed to the World of the Spirit which is made up of Higher Vibrations that though resembling the Earth in many ways cannot really be compared to it, for the realm of the Spirit and those who inhabit it are of such a finer substance, as to be to Mortal eyes what you can term "Invisible" in the sense that Man has not yet opened up his inner senses of perception with regard to what is all around him, and yes part of him, there are those beings who you call Clairvoyants who do have a certain ability and rapor with those who inhabit the Spirit world, but it is of a somewhat limited nature, which is incidentally for Man's own good, in his present state of evolution, too much, too soon, would create havoc amongst the majority of the population and so it is restricted to those who are the gifted ones that we spoke of!!

And now back to the "Mind" that all important element that we take with us wherever we go, and here we are talking in terms of transition, and that does not just apply to the earthly one but to All of them when it is necessary in the evolutionary cycle!!! The Mind as such cannot be observed as it were by sight either by physical or spiritual. We do not wish to confuse you but it is of an essence that is so fine and originates from the Creative Principle you know as God the Creator. Mind essence is the very Thought of that Creator and we have been endowed with that part that is real and yet cannot be observed other than by the inner senses of all known bodies that go to make up what you upon the Earth plane call The Soul! Which is, Pure Mind essence in its original state of being but not knowing of its true potential and its relationship to the Almighty. It has the gift to create which it has to be taught how to use and that is by Thought!! Upon the Plane known as the Soul plane dwell the "Higher Spirits" that are the keepers of the Soul and incidentally the teachers of that one as well!! They are part of the Hierarchy of the Beings of light that have Never touched the lower planes, for their Purity must never be contaminated by those lower vibrations, and yet they are aware of the effects that those lower vibrations have upon the various Spirit essences that are needed by the Soul in its search for its true identity which also includes the physical beings that the Spirit "takes over" for a limited period upon the Earth plane!! So that Mind essence, or we should say Part's of that mind essence vibrate on all the various levels that the Spirit is heir to in its search for its hidden identity that it knows it belongs to and that hidden identity, you know of as the God Creator of all seen and unseen known and unknown aspects of Life, as it is observed on all the various spheres that we gravitate to on our long journey back to our Source of creation!

This journey though long and sometimes arduous and yes somewhat repetitive in its re-incarnating cycles, has No length of Time to the One who is Timeless. Our knowledge of time is but an illusion, but a necessary one if we are to progress, but in reality it is of no importance when we view Eternity as our eventual dwelling place, where Past, Present, and Future, are all ONE!! The NOW!! We will understand that one day and by then it will not be relevant and will not matter at all!!! For then we will be part of who we belong to. Our journey of one life's cycle over and a new and more important one awaits us. And here is where we are told we can go no further in this discourse of the Mind. But remember that the Mind is the Creator of Thought, it is that which is the giver and sustainer of all life forms of both Man's physical and Spiritual nature. Man is unique in that respect because of his freedom of will, that is not known about in the rest of the animal kingdom! So use your Mind wisely for a thoughtless thought cannot be retrieved as easily as it was created!!!

We leave you with that thought, and may the Blessings of those on High be with you now and always on your journey of life. Farewell little travellers on the pathway of discovery Farewell.

And to you Brother Scribe we greet you and leave you in Love and understanding on your journey of discovery, continue with your studies for they are of importance and not only to yourself but to others as well. Farewell dear friend. Farewell.

Chapter 48

November 9th 2004 1.40 a.m.

TWO THAT MERGE AS ONE, EVENTUALLY

Have you ever wondered just what is the relationship between the Physical Body and that of the Spirit? We hear a lot about why the Spirit has to come to the Earth plane to learn lessons and it is through this physical body that enables it to do this, but what about the effect of all of this living has upon the physical part of this relationship of these two separate bodies that are "tied" as it were together for the lifetime of the physical body?! When that brief span has ended with the demise of the body of physical origin what has that one "gained" from this partnership? The Spirit we know continues "its" life once more upon the Spirit plane, and the physical body that was its constant companion is now just a "memory". No longer a body, its usefulness has ended! Does that seem fair I wonder? For after all the physical body has been the main reason for the Spirit's sojourn upon the Earth plane, and that one seems to be the one that reaps all the rewards, while the Mortal body relinquishes its life with nothing as it were to show for it!!! All rather one sided when looked at it like that, so then let us see if the physical vehicle does have any recompense for allowing the Spirit to be part of its life and all that that entails!!

I expect most people if asked would say "Well the mortal body has lived its life upon Earth and that is reward enough isn't it?"

Yes, that is one way of looking at it, but when that lifespan ends, the physical body once more reduced to ashes, it doesn't seem that it has had a fair deal in this partnership does it? All of the efforts of living and striving, getting through life with all of its problems as well as its virtues and for what? Just so that the Spiritual side of this duo can look back over this period and say "Well I've learnt that lesson and I'm now better for having made this journey once again. Wonder who I will be in partnership with the next time I come back to Earth for more tuition in my searching for the reasons that I need to find out more about myself"!!!

So it would seem that the Spirit has gained a great deal out of this liaison of the two bodies doesn't it? You may argue that the physical body has also gained quite a lot, a family that it belongs to and grows up with, and perhaps creates a family of its own and all that that entails in the course of its life, but in the "end" that is it. "The End"!! No longer a body but a fond memory to those who it leaves behind!! But its Spiritual part goes on living for ever!! Still identifiable for a period as the one that it had as its partner upon Earth!!! And if and when it feels it needs to re-incarnate once more upon Earth it will search out once more a suitable vehicle in which to dwell again!! And so the cycle of birth life and death once more begins. With yet another willing participant even if that participant is originally unaware of its prime reason for being brought into existence for the benefit of the Spirit!!!!

It would appear that the Spirit has a great deal to thank its chosen partner in this enterprise of learning how to live upon Earth, for without its companion of the flesh, it could not succeed in this venture could it? So the two are a very, very necessary combination if the Spirit is to benefit from these visits that it has to make upon Earth in its journey of discovery who it really is!!!

So the physical side of this partnership is really one of true unselfishness for it will never really know what it has meant to its spirit partner, only that because of this joining of the two forces the Spirit can continue on its quest for its true identity, eventually to return to the Godhead, with all of the knowledge gained through the lives it has led upon the Earth plane with all of its various physical counterparts that have made it what it now is!!!

So being a physical human being is a great responsibility isn't it? For it is through that relationship with the Spirit that gives the true meaning to that life upon Earth. Perhaps in time we will become more aware of this relationship and the two bodies of existence will know and understand just how much this relationship really means to each of them! Then the true meaning of life will be apparent, Gods will, will be done!! Perhaps one day, then Spirit and Physical will live on both planes of existence not just for one lifetime but for always!!!

Earth will have served its purpose and Spirit will no longer need to live upon it to gain the experience it needs in its evolutionary cycle of upward progression!!! And here is where we part company from this nights discourse, we hope that you dear friends upon the Earth will see yourselves in a fresh light, and know that you are important to both the physical and Spiritual side of your dual nature. We bid you Farewell.

And to you little Brother we wish you well and know that we have all of your interests at heart, God bless and keep you safe little one. Farewell.

Chapter 49

November 11 2004 1.30 a.m.

THE HEAVEN AND WHAT IT HOLDS

When you gaze up to the Heavens and see the twinkling stars, and then begin to realize the sheer vastness of the Universe, where Space seems to go on forever and ever never ending, and then you look around you at your own little World, and then think in terms of the part of this world that you inhabit, do you stop and wonder just what part, you that is the physical you, what part is it that you play in this vast Arena of what we call Life?!!! Out there, in the blackness of Space, where your scientists try to probe for signs of life that might have existed, and perhaps still does that can be identified as "beings" that we could say resemble us upon this Earth?!!! We long to know that we that is we upon Earth are not the only species of human beings that exist in this Universe that has no beginning and no end!!

We long to discover that there are other forms of life, and yet we are apprehensive in case if we do discover them, they may not resemble us at all! And how would we cope with what we like to call Alien life forms!! Those fiction writers upon Earth like to paint pictures of strange looking not quite human like people who might inhabit Planets that at present we have no knowledge of! And most of the, it seems, according to these writers, are anxious to "take over" this planet of ours and make slaves of the present populations!

If there is life out there why should it be so different to ours upon Earth? If you accept God and how he said "Let us make Man in our own image" and if we are the result of this experiment, why should others be any different from US!!? I expect those of a scientific nature will say, if there is life upon other planets, then because they exist so much further out in space, they must vibrate at a much higher and faster rate than we do upon Earth, so there is every likelihood that they the inhabitants of those planets would differ from us Earth beings. Probably lighter in structure that is our bone structure and probably what organs that are within their bodies, would also be somewhat different!! Could that be the case? We have no way of knowing at present have we?! When you come across a person of the human race who is shall we say a "perfect specimen" of that particular race, then they really are God like in appearance aren't they? And it would seem that perfection has been achieved and there would be no reason to deviate from that blueprint would there?

Or does that only apply to the human races upon the Planet Earth?! Much to think about, especially when we are told that the human body is only part of our "make up". For we are also made primarily of Spirit substance which does not in its pure state resemble a human being, though it does have the ability when it chooses to take on the appearance of the human body of its choice, if that is the one it has chosen to be part of in its learning period upon Earth!! So looking at it from that perspective, it would seem that the idea of other varieties of human like beings might not be so far fetched after all!!

Perhaps upon some of these other Planets that we cannot see, the inhabitants might be what we like to call Spirit beings, for we are told that that is what we really are!! Now that does make us think, that there is so much more to being "a person" than we have so far thought about!! While upon the Earth we have to inhabit a physical vehicle of human substance for identification purposes it seems, because of the denseness of this Planet a Spirit would not be able to function properly without this physical covering of protection, which eventually it has to take leave of when the physical body comes to the end of its life cycle!! Our Spirit then returns to its original homeland, where it no longer needs a physical body of reference!!

So then perhaps we would be in a position to explore those Planets where we would be "accepted" because of our Spirit countenance which would be the same as those whose home that Planet is!!! So that has made me wonder if their Planet is their real one, do they also have a sort of satellite Earth one to which they too have to incarnate upon, as we do to gain the experience of life upon Earth?!!

So is this Universe made up of a mixture of Spirit and Physical Planets? Seen and Unseen?! And do we, when we are back upon our Spirit plane go to similar planes of existence to further our education of the meaning of Life? And are all of these planets sort of linked together, not exactly physically but with Electrical currents of thought waves? And could it be that they belong as it were to the same orbital belt, in other words we couldn't just "pop over" to another planet unless it was in our orbit? Perhaps being able to move about in the Universe only comes when we have become more adult in our way of living and understanding of the working complexities of the Universes life cycles, of the various existing planets!

It would seem that we have a great deal of learning to do if we are to be a living part of this vast concourse of planets and their appendages!!

It looks as if our ideas of what our lives are for, will need re-thinking, for our cycle that takes in numerous incarnations before we are ready to proceed further up the scale of evolution, is but a small part of what the real life has to offer us. We think of Eternity as somewhere beyond our present ability to comprehend exactly what it means, but it would appear that, that is exactly what it is! "Eternity"! that takes in many eternities that are in reality never ending!!! So perhaps one eternity leads onto another one in another dimension!! I wonder if it is all one vast circle of knowledge learned, and knowledge gained and then put to good use?!!

Perhaps this would be a good time to call a halt to all of this talk, that can only be accepted as Hypothetical for you cannot verify any of what we have given to you this night and we cannot give to you proof, that will only come when you are ready to accept it!! So we will bid you Farewell friends upon the Earth. And to you dear Brother we bid you Farewell! And thank you for your time and energy. God's blessings be with you little steward of knowledge, that is being untapped!!! And not only for you dear friend but for others, who also wish to know some of the secrets of Life and their inner meanings!!!

Farewell Brother Farewell!

Chapter 50

November 11th 2004

MY THOUGHTS

ARE SOME DREAMS REALITIES?

These are thoughts of mine that have been brought to the surface because of the previous discourse!!

I wonder if one of our other aspects by which I mean our bodies I wonder if some of them, or perhaps only one of them leads a completely different life to the one that we lead upon Earth? Shall I say one of a more "Spiritual" nature and perhaps sometimes that one makes contact with its Earth bound part of its body, say for arguments sake when we upon Earth are in a deep dream state? And if we are receptive to this influence then perhaps our higher spiritual nature that we know of, but seldom get in touch with, benefits this earth body of ours and we perhaps call it by various names, such as our conscience, our Spirit, our better self!!! Now that makes me wonder if when our physical body dies and releases our spirit, does our Spirit "amalgamate" with this other aspect that I mentioned and the two become ONE, so adding to the Spirits knowledge that it has been acquiring while dwelling in the physical body upon Earth? All very hypothetical I must admit! But perhaps "that one" that dwelt upon that other sphere of existence while we are upon Earth, could account for us feeling that we have done certain "things" before, when we know physically we haven't!! Perhaps also "it" this other aspect of ours can influence our thought mechanism and we wonder just where a particular thought originated form? Is "it" perhaps a form of guide or even "Guardian Angel" that knows us better than we know ourselves? The other day I was lying upon my bed thinking of nothing in particular, and suddenly I thought does this body belong to me? For I seemed to have no sensation of being part of it. It was just "there" and I was still aware of who I was, but I didn't feel any sensation of being "alive" other than my "mind"! It lasted for quite a while and then I got up from the bed and went about my normal activities!! I don't think I've had that experience before!! I wonder if it will be repeated sometime? When the conditions are right, I'm being told, by thought!!!

I wonder just how influential these other aspects of ours are to us upon the Earth plane? And its just occurred to me do "they" associate with each other without my knowledge? There's such a lot about us and our various aspects or bodies if you like, that we are not completely aware of, only for brief spells and then we think was that my imagination or have I been dreaming? Now that brings me to another part of my dream state! I've written this somewhere before, but I'll repeat it here. Now in my "dream" I am leaving a railway station which is not all that big and I go along the road leading out from the station, I turn to my right and go up the road which curves round and I go further up because I know it takes me to the upper part of this town and I know the shops there, there are a number of small roads or alleyways leading off each other and there are a number of shops mainly of the antique variety, I look in the window and sometimes go inside, the merchandise is altered so I'm always surprised at what I see. The shopkeepers seem to know me, though I never buy anything I pick things up and put them down again, I wander on, and there's a sort of open market which has areas or yards leading off it, these have what I call second hand goods and sometimes architectural pieces from houses which are interesting, there are lots of people milling around but I don't think they are aware of me! There's a large single story bookshop, actually it seems to sell mostly magazines, I look at them and handle them but do not buy anything. I think somewhere there's a sort of café, because I have eaten cake's from it, I don't know about drinks, I think its tea or coffee! As it seems to be getting dark and the lights are going on I think I had better get back to the Station. I believe there is a "short cut" through this part of the town, but I've never used it, I stick to the road that I came up by. This "town" is not one that, "I", that is me personally have ever been to in "real life" and yet I always know where "everything" is each time I go there in my dreams!!! Wonder if it is "Me" or that other one?!!! Would be interesting to find out!!! Well so much for that little excursion into one of my dream states. There are others that I am familiar with and some of them "go back" years and yet I haven't forgotten them so they must have made an impression upon my mind!! Even just writing this, memories of places keep popping up and the details are still fresh, but I won't bore you with them!!! But "things" are not as straight forward as we think they are, and here I'm referring to what constitutes our life span upon Earth!!

Some people think that this Earth life is all a dream, well if it is, it's a pretty practical one as far as I'm concerned. And doing all of this writing is far from being dream like I can assure you! For at times my "pen hand" gets quite tired of grasping the pen!!! Now has all of this "got me" anywhere? Well I'll have to think about it later, probably after I've recorded it, because when I listen to what I've written it seems to make more sense to me that when I'm writing it!!! I think that, that seems as good a place as any to bring this narrative to a close, so for the time being that is exactly what I'm about to do, so I'll say goodbye or perhaps Farewell sounds less formal and its used a lot by my brothers isn't it? So Farewell it is!!!

Chapter 51

November 13th 2004

ENDANGERED SPECIES!

Let your pen flow little friend, let you pen flow, and our thoughts to become yours. We bring to you peace and the love of your Brothers in Christ.

We begin, fellow travellers we greet you in the name of Jesus the Christ and in His name we will endeavour to enlighten you regarding your journey upon the pathway of life, which incidentally is the journey we all have to make at sometime in our various incarnated bodies of Mortal man. Our host while we tarry upon that sphere of darkness that you call the Earth!

For to us who have been upon the Higher realms of Spirit, where Light pervades our very souls, your Earth, your World, to us is not only dark and oppressive but somewhat sinister at times. And by "Dark" we refer to the cloud that encircles your globe a cloud so dense with all of the thoughts of hatred that is being generated at this period of your History, and those thoughts and actions that stem from them attract from the regions of degeneration even more thoughts that fester and multiply!! You talk of your global warming, and the erratic behaviour of your weather patterns, and you put it down partly to Man's disregard for Nature's role in the stability of this your globe! But it is not only his disregard of her wishes, its his very attempts at trying to bend her to his will! And this has resulted in dire consequences to your way of life! You are No match for Nature when she decides to show you that when flouted she can be a cruel mistress.

It is her way of trying to cleanse the very poisons that you allow to penetrate the fabric of the earth, and the poisons you leach into your streams that empty their filth into the oceans killing the very life that has helped to sustain you through the centuries!!! Within a matter of a few short years you undo what it has taken millenniums to create. Your forests, devastated, your wild life seeking sanctuary and finding none, die, to be no more, and you talk of endangered species, have you not yet understood that Man himself can be numbered amongst them if he is not careful!

Stop this desire to make others bend to your will. You are not God and by the look of it Never will be!! Try and live in peace, and that starts within yourself!! Learn to tolerate what at first you do not understand, and here we are talking not to just one Nation but to All Nations. You are all at fault for you do not follow the precepts of your so called Religious Faiths! You twist them to suit your vile purposes and then have the gall to call upon your God to bless your endeavours!!! We call that Blasphemy!! Have you no shame you people of the Earth, with one hand to hold it out in friendship, while in the other behind your back you grasp a sword!! And you know what is said regarding living by the sword, you will also perish by it!!! Think before you act, and then Think again before you shed innocent blood in vain glorious deeds that end in tragedy. These are the thoughts and deeds that have created that cloud of despair that circlers your Earth. This earth, this World, was created for the benefit of All not just for the so called victorious few!! You try to portray war as some sort of dreadful game, if you could only see the poor wretches that are hurtled into oblivion, limbs torn apart and Spirits broken! And We have to try and mend those poor, poor souls when they awake upon our plane, bewildered and shattered at what they have been a part of!! Our hospitals are overflowing just as yours upon Earth are, such waste and for what? So called Honour? What a hollow sounding word, when the price paid for it is written in Blood, and innocent blood at that!!

Try and instil in your Youth the futility of War and its aftermath. Don't go on year after year saying it must never happen again and then you start preparing for another one just in case!! No wonder your youth have very little respect for their so called elders. This world belongs to them as well as the adults who spawned them, and the adults are on their way out, make no mistake about that, so it will be left to the young to make this World a better place for those who will follow them. The past is past, the future is the future, it is the Now that is important, make of this Now something that generations can look back and say "Well they did their best and we can thank them for that"!

But it has to start somewhere so why not Now? If you really want to make a difference then now is the time to make that effort, forget going to the Moon and beyond, start with this your homeland, your Earth, use your money wisely, don't let famine rule your lives, spread your wealth around, for your real wealth are your children and their children and yes even their children, make sure that, that, can become a reality and not just a wishful dream!

Remember God is the God of All peoples everywhere, share your love of Him with each other and see how you can make of this world one of Gods many Mansions, a Heaven upon Earth! Your Heaven! You don't have to die for it, Live for it. It's all up to you!!

We bid you our customary Farewell, and to you little Scribe, not quite what you expected when we said let your pen flow is it? We give you our Love and our thanks, Farewell little patient friend Farewell.

Chapter 52

November 14 2004 4.35 a.m.

YOUR TRANSITION AND HOMECOMING!

When you first enter the Spirit World after the transition of the body, the thing that strikes you is the Light. There is nothing like it upon Earth that can prepare you for the sheer beauty of it! It is like walking through the heart of a Rainbow!! The vapours simply swirl around you as if to embrace you with a feeling of pure love, each colour, and there are many of them for each hue seems to be made up of many colours, yet each one seems as if it is separate and yet they are all part of the main one, you seem to glide through this aura of living light which also emits sounds that are of such a heavenly quality that all else seems to fade into the distance. You seem to be an "actual part" of all that surrounds you, you are the sound, you are each and every colour, and as you pass through each one so your Spirit body responds with a sensation of exquisite happiness, you feel refreshed and nourished as never before, you are home and at peace and the Love that is all around you is from those who have gone before you and have longed for this reunion! You actually float upon this sea of pure love, voices are not only with you but seem to come from within you as well, for you are now part of all that there is, and so you give yourself up to the sheer wonderment of being once more with all those who you have loved and who have watched over you with such tenderness while you remained upon the Earth, and now you are once more together and you sink into a deep sleep of thankfulness and when you awake your new life is spread before you, you see and feel it, it is like a kaleidoscope of many aspects of what this new experience is, and you know that this Heaven that you are now in is just part of what has been promised you and is now a true reality!!!

All of this is somewhat like a beautiful dream and is for the purpose of your adjustment to this dimension of Thought and how it can now be used in your coming life upon this plane.

You can now just accept all that is placed before you, the choice is yours and a new vista opens up. This then, is the life that is yours to make of it what you will, there are so many alternatives for you to choose from, and each one will benefit you Spiritually, for you now are truly Spirit in every sense of the word, but this is not a dream world, it is a world of reality, one where a place is waiting for you, first though you must get to know who you really are, who you have become through your sojourn upon Earth, which seems so long ago now, almost as if it never existed. But it did and what you learnt while upon that dense planet has been of use to you, it has helped to make you who you now are!

You will soon be ready to step out on your own, for you are now a part of all that you perceive, you will be taken on a journey, first though, for your new life will not be confined to just one area of this world of the Spirit! You will find much of what you see and encounter will be familiar to you, for this is not the first time that you have been here, and you may find that you can "pick up" where you left off when last you were here, friendships that you made can now be revived and perhaps projects that were left unfinished can once more be re started! Life you will find is so full and exciting in every way, you have matured since the last time you were here and so you have much to give to those around you, you may still have much to learn, but you have all the time in the world in which to do it!!

This then is your real and true life, and it is up to you what you make of it! So go forward and enjoy it, for you have earned this reward by being who you are and who you will become!!!

We bid you Farewell dear friends for this has been but a brief glimpse of what the future life holds for you all.

Farewell and God's blessing go with you. And you dear Brother, peace be with you and know that we give you our love and our blessings.

Farewell little scribe, Farewell.

Chapter 53

November 17th 2004 3.00 a.m.

UNIVERSAL LOVE AND WHAT IT CAN ACHIEVE

Just what is our objective in life? To just get through it somehow or to use each day as a gift that has been bestowed upon us by a benign being that we call God? Whichever way you look upon it, it amounts to the same thing. We are Alive, and we are living!!! But living varies such a lot depending on who you are and where you are, in what we think of as Our World!! If you are one of the fortunate ones who live in a part of the world that is relatively free from want, then life can be sweet, but what about those people who are subjected to hardship and poverty and there seems to be millions of them all over this planet today, their lives are hardly what you could term "sweet" are they?

So why all of this inequality between the races? It seems so unfair doesn't it? And why you wonder, why should there be such a difference, depending upon where you live and what particular race you belong to!!!

Is it just luck or is there a logical reason for this discrepancy in the lives of those who dwell upon this lower planet we call Earth? It would seem that that adage called "Survival of the fittest" must be the answer! And yet why should that be? If as we are told we are all children of the one God? You would think that, if that is true then we should all be given the same opportunities regarding this life that we are living. But it doesn't work out like that does it?

And "Why" you wonder, and who decided what? Looking at it from an outsiders point of view it does seem to be biased in certain countries favour doesn't it? And that is bound to set up a conflict of who is to Have and who will end up as a Have Not!!!

There just does not seem to be a fair and logical answer does there? Yet there is an answer and a very good one and it is in one word Sharing!! Sharing what those who have an abundance of, what might be called the basic necessities of life, with those who are being starved of them, literally!! If we are all Brothers and Sisters, then we should act as a loving family of Nations towards each other and not as we are at this present time in the Worlds cycle of evolution. With eyes of hostility and yes greed. For that word is at the root of all of the unhappiness and unfairness that abounds upon this lower planet! Yet there is enough of everything to go round if it was distributed fairly and not with a price tag attached to it!!! Can't you see that if those who have plenty, shared it with those who lack it there would be harmony in the world. War would cease to be the only answer that so many Nations resort to, to get their own way, regardless of how it affects those who are at the mercy of those stronger Nations, who it seems use their strength to subdue instead of helping the weaker ones to gain strength and become independent of what the stronger Nations dare to call their bounty, which is not given freely, but usually with some hidden agenda which means even more hardship for those recipients in the long run!!!

Man must wake up to his responsibility towards his fellow Man, why do you think that you are considered by Those who dwell upon the distant planets, as Barbarians? And not worth cultivating as equals, which you upon Earth are certainly not. You are a selfish breed of human beings and not worthy of the name human!! You are if you did but realize it very, very low down on the scale of Cosmic Evolution!! That is why you are still Earth bound when you should be upon the upward path towards those other Planets that have been where you are now, but who have advanced because they have learned the lesson's that were put before them and yes overcame them and what with? With Love, which is what is sadly lacking upon your dense planet, we can see what your Earth could become if you were to live by that principle and we can also see what would happen to it if you don't! A warning to you, before it is too late. There was a time when you were NOT! And that could easily become your fate once more if you do not learn to live in Harmony, not only with each other but also with Nature who can be a willing servant if treated properly, but can also become a hard task master if abused!!!

We want to help you to become part of the Universal Brotherhood of Nations, not only upon your Earth but part of what you know as the Universe. For it is teeming with life, that you have absolutely no idea about, and yet it is there and has always been, but your eyes have been closed to what is all around you, and we speak not of those eyes of sight, but the eyes of inner perception, when you learn how to "see" with them, then you will know that you are truly making progress in the right direction!! This cannot come about "overnight" so to speak, and it will need hard work and discipline upon your part but the rewards that await you, if you could see them would astonish you! Start now, make an effort to try and understand each other, accept the differences and build upon those differences for they are not insurmountable, they are the very essence of a successful life!! You have much to learn you children of the Earth but we that is those of us upon the Higher realms of existence are patient, for we are you Elder Brothers and the message we leave with you this night is Love, learn to live with it and also learn to share it, for Love really is the answer to all of life's problems. And Love means giving of yourself freely, mind, body and Soul. There is no other way, but it is the only way if you are to fulfil God's plan that you are still a part of!!!

And here is where we depart from you, friends upon the Earth. We do care about you and we will help you, if you will let us!! Farewell and Peace be with you. And to you little person Farewell, we do know of you!! And our Love we send to you. Farewell.

Chapter 54

December 1st 2004 1.00 a.m.

THE ECCENTRICITY OF TIME!

Dear Brethren of the Earth! We say to you TIME! And what does that word mean to you? 24 hours, a day, a week, a month, even a year!! But just what is it? Can you catch it and put it in your pocket to bring out later and say look! This is a piece of time?!! You cannot see it and yet you are always aware of it and it's significance in your life!! So just what is this illusive thing that to some is so important, while to others it is a burden, a burden of despair!!!

Each of us "sees" time differently depending on the degree of importance that we attach to it!! A student may find that he has not enough of it while he is pursuing his studies, while one who is elderly and perhaps infirm would give anything for the passage of time to fly past, where an hour becomes a minute and not the age that it seems to take when counting up the minutes the hours and the days!!! So then what can we make of this thing we call "time"? It really is entirely up to the individual isn't it? But it doesn't stop there, for "time" belongs to everyone and not just to a few!! It would seem that we are governed by it, and have no say in the matter!

But stop and think about if for awhile! And here we do not talk about the job aspect where time as such is sometimes like an enemy and not a friend! We will concentrate on what you could call "your leisure time", where time is now your servant and not your master!! How do you use this wonderful commodity that is at your disposal? Well! How do you use it? Do you use it profitably or do you just fritter it away until it is time for either your sleep state or even back to your place of work?!!

Time is NOT what it may seem, for in some areas in your Universe time as you know it does not exist!! It is timeless, for upon some planets time is not relevant, it is neither yesterday nor today nor even the future it is the eternal NOW. And how can that be you wonder, you just cannot envisage what the NOW means!! Some might say it is past present and future all rolled into one!! Does that mean then that there wasn't a past that would bring us to today and that today would be the future? Too much for our physical brains to try and unravel, for we live in another dimension to some of those other planes of existence! Just think about the phrase "Light years away" and what we may be seeing is no longer a reality as we know it!!!

And when you talk about planets and worlds that are million's and millions of earth miles away!! Supposing that our term "earth miles" cannot really mean "their miles". For if we could be in their dimension then who knows, we could be living in their past or even their future and yet physically perhaps they no longer exist, we are just "seeing" a memory of what was and no longer is!! So perhaps Space may be less populated by these planets and worlds than we realize!! They may even represent an illusion that like, a mirage upon Earth represents something real that is not in the actual vicinity but many, many miles away and even then may only be a sort of photographic memory that was a reality once but no longer is!! So, could that be that what the scientists tell us about these planets that they wish to explore in outer space are no longer there, so what will be the outcome of these voyages of discovery that result in an illusion of reality that now does not exist?!!

We are back once again to this times scale aren't we? If we are not careful we may find that those who are the explorers of the future may find themselves in a "time scale" that is alien to them and that could play havoc with their Minds and yes even their physical bodies, so that they may start out shall we say in their 20th year and find themselves still 20, but actually in their 40th year of earth time or even older?!! And how will that affect their bodies on their return to Earth?!! Perhaps we had better not pursue that subject further for the consequences might not be acceptable to today's thinking!!

We can now proceed to the "Dreamstate" where as you know time as such is topsy-turvy to say the least, as an example, you may in your dream be walking down a street say, today and before you have taken more than a dozen steps it is now tomorrow and the whole scene could have changed and yet it all seems quite normal and you do not query it! Time in dreams mean absolutely nothing in terms of reality and yet it is easily accepted, so what then if our "waking life" would turn out to be similar? Would we then accept that "today" was "tomorrow" or even "yesterday" or even the Now!! And so go along with it? Now if Dreams and reality, this is waking reality merge one day into one, what then would be our conception of Time!! Would it no longer be relevant to our lives and we would then exist in a "Timeless Zone" upon a physical world that no longer relied upon time as a necessity or even as a commodity to be used?!!!

Perhaps this is a "good time" to draw this discourse upon time and it's eccentricity to a close before we confuse you any more for all of this assumption is purely hypothetical on our part, but it may make you think about time and how you spend it!! And so we will bid you Farewell little earth students, and give you time to think about what has been said!!

And to you little Brother Scribe we bid you Farewell and hope we have stimulated your thought patterns, though we can tell you that whatever conclusions you come to regarding the passage of time, you upon earth at present will not be able to alter it!!! Farewell Brother Farewell!!! Till next Time!!!!

Chapter 55

December 2004 2.45 a.m.

THE ETERNAL

We greet you in Love. Peace be with you all!!

When you think of Eternity, that is if you ever do! And let us face it very few people even think as far ahead as that word implies!! Well what comes into your mind when you see that word in print? It is rather awesome is it not? We can think of today and even yesterday and maybe tomorrow and yes even shall we say the "future"! but it tends to end there doesn't it? For beyond that there looms the spectre of death of the mortal body and to many people that's it!!! To others there is the prospect of a "new life" one that starts upon the world, people like to call the Spirit one! And to many people who may think along those lines, that is the answer they have always looked for that satisfies their curiosity. But do they ever stop to think what might lie beyond the Spirit World that they have read about and have been told about by those people who are what are called "clairvoyants"! Does anyone really know about "Eternity" and what it is that we belong to? For we know that our "Spirit" never "dies" in the sense that we think of regarding the mortal body! The Spirit is part of the Eternal force of Life itself. In other words, an aspect of the "God Creator, the Eternal One", that has always been and always will be, For the Eternal is another expression of the word Eternity! Eternity is where we are, even at present we can never escape it, for our "Spirit Self" that part of us that is also a part of our Creator is "forever"! Do not think in terms of the "human self" which only lasts for one lifetime and then physically is no more! What it has accomplished during that brief span upon Earth can be a legacy left behind for others to appreciate and yes "build upon" and here we are talking in broad terms, the leaders of Nations, the inventors, the Artists, all those who contribute to the lives of those people who are touched by those who we could call gifted, and that word can be taken either way if you so wish, for "gifts" can be used and also abused and we leave that there and proceed further. What humanity does or does not do upon this planet called Earth applies only to it in this phase of its evolution!

It does not impinge upon the unknown areas of this your Universe. In time it may, but that is not our concern in this discourse. We will say though, that the word "Eternity" may be more flexible than you think! Depending upon which Universe you belong to!!! Now that will give you food for thought, for "your" Universe is one of many and not the only one in existence, and we might add it may not necessarily be the only one that you will dwell upon during your spell in the realms of the Eternal!!

Think carefully about what we are saying and know that it does not apply to all entities known as Spirit!!! Like all things to do with the Spirit and its Human counterpart, progress depends upon the individual, and as you know not all individuals progress either at the same pace or even in the same "direction"!! By which you may gather that not everyone wishes to venture beyond the perimeter of their known Universe, they can remain in their "section" of the Eternal for as long as they wish and that to them would be their "Eternity"!!! While to the more adventurous they would view this ongoing Eternity upon another planet in another Universe as the beginning of a "new life" with perhaps entities hitherto unknown to them, but who all belong to the same Universal Force of Life that governs All of Creation in its many and varied aspects and we speak not only of Planets and Worlds but also of those who occupy them!!

The Act of Creation and Creativity is far more complex than

has hitherto been understood, "it" does NOT just come about of its own volition. Thought from the "Creator Mind" is the governing factor and like all forms of creation, perfection is the ultimate aim in this "creating" and so you will understand that the word "experimentation" plays a big part in the furtherance of this creative principle!! Which we will add is a "Collective form of Creation" by those who are the designated Creators in this ongoing Creative enterprise of the Eternal Mind principle, that has No Name that could possibly describe what cannot be described, but only understood by the "inner feelings" of those "Most High". And here we talk of "beings of Light" that do NOT exist in any known Universe, for they are beyond those creations, and where they dwell and have their domain we are forbidden to speak of. A mystery that will forever remain as such.

So do not think, little people of the Earth that you will be able to unravel such a mystery, for it is even beyond our vast intelligence and we speak of a fact, so accept what we have said. You have been given much, this meeting of the mind of that person with the instrument that writes! Sift through the information you have been given, and accept what you can and leave alone for the time being what may seem to you as beyond your present understanding.

Before we leave you, just remember what we have said about "Eternity being flexible"!! And think about it and know that it is a truth that we have told you!!! Even if you cannot verify it for yourself. And so we will say to you Farewell brethren of the Earth.

To you Dear Brother we hold out a hand of friendship, and know that your work is appreciated. Farewell and May the Blessings of the Ones from on High be with you now and always. Farewell little Scribe, yours is a lonely path that you have chosen to tread, but the rewards at the end of it are all the more sweet because of your sacrifice. Farewell. Farewell.

Chapter 56

December 6th 2004

CREATION IS FOREVER ONGOING

We speak of Thoughts, about Light Crystals of differing magnetic strengths and colours that join together, and also repel each other, they form the "building blocks" of life itself! They are minute bundles of pure energy, they can be separated and used in their colour combinations. And by separation we mean the magnetic force of attraction can cause shall we say small explosions when two or more of these light crystals meet and as they explode and separate they form still more crystals not always of light, some become a form of liquid that can be used and stored when known how to, and this "liquid" also generates magnetic force and swirls about in a hectic manner until it finds its "partner" and then it joins together forming a liquid ball of Pure Light energy which floats around until it gets amalgamated with similar balls of light, this procedure goes on and on until eventually it becomes a "power house" attracting other forms of energy to itself and as these forms grow and grow and multiply they become the genes that create a planet that can in time become suitable for habitation! Not at first of humanity that comes much, much later, when all the light crystal's have become what you would call an Earth, like substance, still vibrating and giving off waves of other forms of electrical vibrations that are the nucleus of life creations, they gradually build up what is known as your foliage, your trees, all life stems from these crystals that are no longer seen as separate light emanations, and yet they still are separate if you were to split them open, they would not die but amalgamate with other crystals of life force, and so become a form of mutation, for example a new species of life form!! That would not necessarily resemble the original concept that was first started out when they were attracted to each other!! All forms of "Life Force" are made of the same substance, that is why the Electrical discharges from various plant growth can become toxic to man if he is not careful, but he can actually "tame" this flow and when diluted can be used in the medical field to combat certain viruses that are ever present in the atmosphere!! Life force can be used to promote life or on the other hand can be used to destroy it!!! Man has a choice as he always has had and it is up to him to chose the right course of action if he wishes to progress upon his chosen planet of habitation!

Now all of this that we have written covers millions and millions of so called years of evolution and does not always result in what you might call a "liveable environment"! that is for Man!! But it could well sustain life forms that could tolerate these strange variations. All of this "force of Life" is Monitored, and adjusted according to circumstances that may prevail!! Those beings who do this monitoring and yes adjusting of these life patterns are known as the "true administrators" and their law is the law and cannot be altered unless they give permission!! You could call them Gods but they are minor ones in the overall scheme of the Creative Principle of Life itself!! The Hierarchy of those who Create is in a form of "tiers" one above the other, sometimes overlapping but not very often Creation is not as straight forward as one might think, and mistakes have been made and probably will still be made, which is quite understandable when experimentation is under way!! Error is allowed and permitted by those in the Higher Authority but only up to a certain point and will not be tolerated if it should be seen to be the result of thoughtless actions!!

We leave you here and will resume at a later date.

We resume! "Man" and here we speak of all other forms of Mankind, male and female are not necessarily of the same species that you belong to upon the planet known as "Earth"!! As we have previously said there is always ongoing Creation and experimentation and all that that implies!! But do not think that other forms of what you call the "humanities" are mutations of the original species! They are original in their own right. They may vary in structure from your species, but that is because of basic improvements that have been well thought out and planned, and yet you would have no difficulty in recognising them as belonging to what you would call the "human race" As they in their turn would accept you as belonging to another group, but still part of their orbital belt of planetary expansion!!! Here we are speaking of those planets and their inhabitants that exist Now in this Universe, future ones we will not elaborate on in this discussion!! Just accept, that all forms of the humanities are made up of physical and more importantly Spirit essence, now this Spirit Essence is Universal in its identification of form, in other words Spirit is Spirit wherever it happens to be, you are all the Same in that aspect, it is only when you come down to the human physical body that you differ from each other!! And that of course depends upon your particular planet of existence and where it is to be found in the living fabric of the Universe!!! And here we are only speaking of your and our Universe and not those others that exist beyond the outer limits of our known one!!!

The Whole of Creation defies description, for it is forever ongoing and never ceases, even when perhaps a Universe and its planetary contents are in a form of slumber awaiting the Breath of the Divine to animate it once more into life!! There will come a time when Universes will be able to be part of each other, still retaining their own and original identity, but merging in their relationship with those Creators who monitor their life patterns.

Then certain Universes will amalgamate with others of similar construction and the whole cycle of birth and re-birth will begin again but this time on Higher Vibrations, where Earth's no longer exist as planes of learning, for the beings that now inhabit those higher planets and worlds are Pure Spirit and physical incarnations are no longer necessary to them! They have reached Perfection in every sense and are ready to be true co-workers with their Creator Gods. And so the circle once more begins a cycle of evolution, for those yet to be created and born are nurtured by those whose journey of discovery has brought them to this point, where they are able to be the guides and helpers for those in need of their love and understanding.

So we are back to where we started. But with a deeper understanding of some of the mysteries of Creation and its Creators and those who are created, You, and Me, All of Us, who belong to the one we call OUR GOD!

We feel that we have given you quite enough for you to think about, but remember we are not infallible, accept what you feel you can, don't reject what you do not understand, just put it aside for the time being and come back to it at a later date! We bid you students upon the Earth Farewell and may you receive God's blessings in abundance.

To you Little Scribe, we give you our love and know that we do watch over you always. Farewell dear friend Farewell.

Chapter 57

December 7th 2004 2.30 a.m.

THE UNIVERSE DEFIES DESCRIPTION

What is it that we shall talk about tonight? Something that will give you food for thought and that is:- The Universe! Such a vast subject and how can we approach it? And from what angle? We tend to look upon the Universe as some gigantic sphere of Space, which contains multitudes of stars, planets, worlds and of course cosmic debri!! Which is usually the "leftovers" from planets that no longer exist!! So how can we view this area of Space that contains so much? And does it actually contain as much as we think it does? In a way that Space is almost like a black mirror reflecting what we do not actually see in reality!! Rather a puzzle is it not? For if it is a reflection that we see then somewhere there must be the reality existing, but where? Scientists talk about millions of miles and light years away as if we upon this little planet can actually judge that distance with any form of accuracy! For Space does not just remain as an empty void of nothingness, it is forever expanding and contracting and yes squeezing what it holds in its grasp!! Our Universe is Alive just as we are, it breathes it moves, it even slumbers, it is like a gigantic body that needs feeding to sustain its life force! Just like our bodies, with our arteries that are the highways and byways that carry our life giving blood to the very heart of our living body, and so the Universe is the same, only on a scale that we can hardly imagine!! It too has its arteries that criss cross its whole body, but these arteries are for the benefit of those Planets and Worlds, they are pathways that can lead to the very worlds that we seek and yet cannot find!

If you could spread the Universe upon a flat surface you would be able to see these pathways, they form a map of guidance, but we as yet do not know how to read it!! Others have, and they are of the Planets of cosmic understanding, they watch and wait to see if those upon the distant Planet of Earth have the ability to plot a course that will bring them face to face with those who they seek, and hope to find another species of Mankind like themselves!! At present that is not possible, for we upon Earth do not have the facilities to accomplish this feat. And it will avail us nothing to try and venture upon Planets that cannot sustain life as we know it! And in some cases they never have and never will, they are hostile and we will be foolish to waste our time money and energy finding out that that is just what they are HOSTILE!

There are far more worthwhile areas awaiting discovery that could sustain life that is beyond our wildest dreams!! Populations that are so far advanced, not only in their technical achievements but in their thought abilities that would astound us and show us just how backward we really are in comparison with these other Planets of distinction! They know that we are not ready yet, either in our thinking or our behaviour patterns, that would allow us to be on intimate terms with them!! "War" and its aftermaths are the main stumbling blocks that exclude us from being welcomed into the Cosmic Galaxies of advanced civilizations, that have been in existence long, long before our planet was formed!! We are what you might term juveniles to their adulthood. We have a lot of catching up to do if we wish to be part of those other living beings of light that we could eventually call Our Brothers!!! Some of those advanced Planets no longer need Earth style places of learning! They have progressed beyond the mortal being of brief habitation, that we upon Earth have to use to gain the knowledge that we need in our evolutionary progress!!! They are Spirit first and foremost, but unlike us they know who they are and where their place is in the scheme of the "Universal Cosmic Mind Creation". We are learning the hared way, as they once did, as all life forms that reflect the face of the Creator do in their evolutionary cycles of upward progression!!

Spirits if we have to still use that word are usually identified as "human" like in appearance, but that is only one of their many facets of identification, we have the same ability when we resume our stay upon the Spirit realm that adjoins our Earth, but our abilities cannot be compared to theirs we are afraid, but we are making progress and you can believe that for it is the truth. One day we will become as one being only, that is no longer needing a physical body of reference, and then we really will know that we have progressed as it has been planned for us.

The Universe holds many mysteries for us to one day unravel. One of them is this Orbital belt that we all belong to, that is our particular one that is responsible for keeping this world stable. Others planets can move out of their original one when they reach the Higher vibrationary force in their evolutionary progress! A goal that is considered very worthy of the effort they have to put into it to achieve this distinction!

The Universe does not stand still by any means, there is continual movement, that some might call upheaval but it is all ordered and under control in spite of what it might seem like! And talking of the Universe, we would add here that the one we think of as Ours, is not the only one in existence!! There are many more, for the Space our Universe dwells in is so vast and unending that to try and define it is impossible in the language of the Earth!!! For Creation continues wherever there are Creators and you may call them Gods if you wish for that is what they are. The Hierarchy of the Creative life Force continues to grow and is not confined to just a few, though to become part of that elite band of Creators takes in time what you upon earth would call many millenniums!! But then time is not always relevant when dealing in Eternity and the Eternal!!!

When thinking about the Universe has it occurred to you that all that we observe when looking into Space including our own Planet is in fact on the Inside of the Universe, which is like a gigantic ball, which incidentally it is not ball shaped but is oval in appearance and if we are on the inside of this body of cosmic energy, then there must be an outside mustn't there? A sort of skin of protection that protects all Universes that exist in this area of Space that is never ending. If and it is a big If, and entirely hypothetical, if you could float above and outside of our known Universe, you would see below you numerous Universes of varying sizes floating as it were in a sea of pure energy, that defies description for it is somewhat like a "bubbling cauldron" of gaseous substance, hence the need for the protective skin that we mentioned earlier!! Within each Universe there is much activity between the various planets that are in the same orbital belt. In other words they are in constant communication and that includes not only by thought but actual physical exchanges, they travel back and forth, which is relatively easy with their advanced knowledge of transportation!!

Much for you to think about and wonder at, for we in our little World are on the perimeter of the Real World of existence that we like to call Space and that word cannot fully describe what Space actually is!!! And here we feel that we will bring this discussion to a close and allow your little Scribe to rest from his labours!! So we will bid you and him Farewell for the present. And give you God's blessings now and for the days to come. Farewell dear Earth friends Farewell.

Chapter 58

December 8th 2004

THE FORCE FIELD OF LIFE

Electricity!! What can we tell you about it? Upon Earth you see but a fraction of what Electricity is capable of!! Though sometimes when a storm erupts and the thunder and lightning is all to apparent to the senses, you do get a glimpse of some of it's awesome power that is unleashed, yet even that is not all that it is capable of. If only it could be tamed and stored and used as Man desires and not wasted as it is at present and always has been through the ages. Man is waking up to the power of Solar energy at last, and if he puts his thinking cap on he may discover ways of harnessing this untapped force of energy, that could be used for many things including your rather antiquated forms of transport!! Electrical currents would revolutionize your present form of transportation. We know that it is used in some of your cars, but it is not used as it should be to good effect. You could have a form of magnetic strip, somewhat like your cassette tapes, that when it was switched on so to speak would drive your vehicles by computer mechanics, silently, swiftly and with hardly any moveable parts that would need replacing. No form of noisy engine giving off fumes that can cause illness and respiratory problems!!!

One of the reasons that so many people today are suffering from respiratory infections and stress related diseases is because they are more prone to the electrical discharges that are bombarding your Earth from tears in the fabric of the atmosphere! Caused by Man himself we hasten to add!!

As you are aware we, that is our body, is governed by electricity in every thing that we do! The brain is like a battery that is fully charged, just waiting for the right switch to be pulled as it were so that the electrical impulses can be carried along the invisible wires to the required destination where the Brain can put into motion the movements required for any particular effort that is needed!!! All of this requires but a fraction of a second to complete and we just take it for granted!! We are even surrounded by Electrical vapours that penetrate the body at various points and some of these vapours actually help to eliminate toxic elements that are clogging up the nervous system!! Some people can see these vapours that they call the "Auric Field" and can tell the state of the persons health by their various colour combinations!! Perhaps one day the local physicians will be able (after being taught by those who know!) will be able to see this Aura when viewing a patient and so diagnosis will be much easier and safer altogether.

We visualize that also in time, patients in Hospitals will also be treated in this way and there will be no need for aesthetics for the whole body will be put into a form of "suspended animation" which will last for as long as the surgeon thinks it is necessary. And the recovery and healing process will be speeded up by the patient themselves, even if they are unaware of their part in this procedure!!! So you see that implies that all of these electrical charges can be regulated and reversed when deemed necessary. We are surrounded all the time by invisible electrical currents, they are vital to our well being, they are even in the food that we eat. All living forms of creation have this force field around and within them, that is why in the future the vegetables that you will consume will be free from pesticides and any form of additives, for these pesticides etc tend to neutralize the natural flow of electrical magnetism that is part of the life force of these foods. And as for the eating of animal flesh, that also will be a thing of the past, for remember that animals as well as humans all have this electrical force field around and in them and once an animal has been slaughtered that force field of protection ceases and the body in fact starts to disintegrate and the flesh that is eaten has lost its most important asset which is its life force!!!

You will no doubt say "Well that about the vegetables, they are dead aren't they?!" But with vegetation that magnetic force remains within the vegetable for a considerable time, and if it is eaten reasonably fresh, then none of the nutrients are lost!!! Now you can begin to understand how important it is for us to know how to use this life force of ours, that is within and without of this mortal body that we inhabit even only on a temporary basis. In fact this electrical magnetic force field is with us all the time, by which you will know that we are speaking of our Spirit body as well as the physical!

Once upon the Spirit plane all these electrical emanations are far more apparent than they were when we were upon the Earth plane! And they can be "read" and understood quite easily, when you get to know what the various colours that surround another Spirit entity mean!! That is one of the reasons why "speech" is not always needed when you are conversing with another person!! Thought can travel from one to another, when it is regulated and that of course is by Electrical wave lengths and colour co-ordinations!! For colour plays a very important part in all of this Electrical movement. Now you can see why it is we call some of the Higher beings upon the realms of the Spirit, "Beings of Light", for that is exactly what they are, they are not only surrounded by light but it comes from within them also!! They are it would seem a form that is recognisable and yet the light emanations can be so bright and strong that to our eyes they appear like a luminous oval spectrum of living vibrating energy, we can feel it and are enfolded within it and we feel such love and peace entering our body that we are content to remain in that state forever! Of course, we do not, but we have experienced something that we will never forget and even the thought of it revives that feeling of warmth and Love. But remember they are the "Higher Beings of Light" and we do not encounter them all of the time. But when we do!! Well we never forget the meeting ever!!

All of the Planets and their occupants in our Universe are "made up" of Electrical impulses, for Electricity is the very life force of all creation. It is virtually everywhere and in everything. And there is no end to its variations and use's, it can be solid, it can be liquid even, it can be visible and it can be invisible, it is in fact Everything and that includes US!! So remember you people upon the Earth, that you emanate electricity in one way or another and so, when moving into areas where there are many people, surround yourself with your protective shield of Thought, and their varying vibrations will be of no hindrance to you. But don't let that stop you from giving out a healing thought when you see someone perhaps old and bent, or with a sad expression upon their face and yes even those elderly people who have a look of fear in their eyes, they are perhaps bewildered in this day and age of haste and yes uncaring. Just a thought or a smile as you pass them, for quite often their energy field may be very low and your thought does make a difference for it is in fact an electrical current sent with Love.

Here we will bid you Farewell dear friends of the Earth and to you too little scribe.

Chapter 59

December 20th 2004 1.45 a.m.

SCIENCE AND WHAT IT LACKS!

Having watched a television programme last night regarding the Universe or Universe's and Man's place in them I was hoping for some form of enlightenment on the subject, but even after an hour of graphics and theoretical explanations of this and that, I found I had been told nothing! And quite frankly that didn't surprise me. The people interviewed, highly intelligent people with lots of scientific knowledge at their disposal and all sorts of theories for and against and yet not one of them mentioned when speaking of mankind did they even think, that man was anything more than a physical being with a large brain!!! No mention of the Spirit that is part of mans make up!!! Personally I just cannot understand how these scientific people who have spent their whole lifetimes trying to fathom out Mankind and his place in the Universe and they never seem to get any further than the physical human being, that only exists for one lifetime upon Earth and no mention of his lifetimes companion who is an integral part of Man, the one who not only animates him, but is essential to Man's evolution and of course the Spirits also!!! That is the whole point of Man being born upon Earth in the first place as a vehicle for the Spirit to use in its furtherance of its search for its true identity!!

One of these intelligent persons even suggested that we might even be a product of a higher beings computerized brain and that we didn't even exist outside of it!!!! We are in fact, not real at all!!! Oh yes, they did mention God in passing, but they didn't seem at all sure about the existence of such a being!!! And as for the purpose of Man being created for a particular purpose, that too eluded them!!! I just cannot understand their way of thinking, which to me seems very flawed! No mention of what happens when Man's mortal body ceases to exist and all of the knowledge of that lifetimes experience just vanishes, unless of course they were inventors or artists that left a legacy for others to appreciate and profit by!!! And what about the real world of the Spirit to which we all belong and come from in the first place?!! Surely that is worthy of their mental activity in trying to understand the reason for all of life! They seem to think that we are fortunate to be here at all, as if its entirely by chance, and a digit one way or another could have meant that neither we or the Universe would exist!!!

And yet they also seemed to have a secret yearning that somehow somewhere their was an intelligence that may have had a hand in all of this creation business!!! So why haven't they explored the Spirit side of Man, which to me seems to be the only logical explanation of why Man has been created and here the word Man incorporates the Spirit as well, and also the Universe and its various Worlds and Planets that can and do house beings like ourselves!! Plus of course those other Universe's that at present we know nothing about, but who, as far as I am concerned do Exist, and are important to Us in our evolutionary cycle of existence!!! Of course once anyone starts talking about the Spirit side of Life, most of these scientific bodies will just smile and tap their heads and then go about their business of exploring in the wrong direction and wondering why they never come up with a satisfactory answer to their questions!!! They talk of Man's brain and how we possess the intelligence that goes with it, but they don't say that we do not as yet use our brain to its full capacity!! And why? Because we do not take into consideration what influence our Spirit should be using in this enterprise!! Man is not a complete entity if he does not use his Spirit side in his journey of discovery upon Earth, which is primarily for the Spirits benefit, for it is the Spirit that does not die when Man quits his mortal body at death!! The Spirit lives forever while mortal man only lives for one lifetime and then is no more!! And so when the Spirit wishes to re-incarnate once more upon the Earth plane it has to choose another mortal body of convenience to do so!! All very logical and practical if you look at it in the proper way! And that is just the way the scientific bodies seem to fight shy of exploring, that will give them some of the answers to the questions that they are seeking!! When you look at our World, and the Universe it tells you that there must have been Thought behind its construction, it just doesn't come about by an accident of molecular animations that just happens to come together and form what it is that we see around us, including Man himself!!

Thought that is Divine Thought is behind all of Creation and by Divine Thought I am not talking of just ONE Divine Thought but many and that I'm afraid will upset many people who may read this! But if you really stop and think you will know that what I have written is feasible even if it goes against all of your preconceived ideas of God. I for one do not deny the existence of OUR GOD but read that again our god, and that implies that there must be more than one God Creator? And why shouldn't there be? The Universe is big enough for there to be more than just the one that we have been constantly told exists!! But you must be prepared to give up some of your old ways of thinking about Creation and the Creator or Creators who are responsible for it!!! Go on believing and accepting and be prepared to then move forward in your thinking, don't think that because you have always been told that this or that is so that it has to remain that way! Use that wonderful Brain that we've been given and use it wisely, with thought from your Mind that invisible something that goes with you forever, for Thought is behind everything that exists and happens, both from you and from your God Creator!!

And that is where I am going to leave you, Think for yourself and don't accept everything that is told you, yes even what I have written, you don't have to agree with me, but if it sets you thinking then I've done what I was told to do, even though I wasn't aware that I was being used this night by those who I call my Brothers but I'm glad I was. Farewell.

Chapter 60

December 29th 2004

THE JOURNEY

Dear Brother, we are going to take you on a journey. A journey of your Mind and Ours. But we will use more than just our Thoughts to take us and you to where we are going to visit not a hermit, but a Holy Man who knows of our visit to be, that will include you little scribe, yes you, so prepare yourself for a very rare visit to one who is far, far, away!!

And so let us begin this journey. We travel to a distant sphere, not of this World but of Ours. Over land and over sea, above the mountain tops and in the depths of valleys that are hidden from sight. We travel by day and then we travel onwards into the night and then once again as the Sun rises we know that we are nearing our destination.

For there in the distance are the mountains of solitude where our Holy Being of Light awaits our coming.

We come to rest at the base of the mountain that seems to be ringed by a vaporous cloud of palest pink touched by the morning sun with streaks of gold. We look upwards to see where the path that we are on will lead us, it disappears and then reappears only to be lost to view once more, but we know that this is the right path that we must take to reach our goal.

We ascend and find that our steps, as if by magic allow each step that we take to be like an effortless movement, almost as if we are being propelled by unseen hands in a gentle gliding motion. Each new turn of the path gives us a glimpse of a vista that takes our breath away, flowers, birds, creatures we have never seen before, all living in harmony and friendship.

As we near the top of this mountain we are upon a plateau of soft vegetation that has a perfume somewhat like sandle-wood and attar of roses, that is quite heady and intoxicating. At the far end of the plateau is a cave or cavern that has the appearance of a shell and with the suns rays it is turned into a golden shrine.

We approach for as yet we have not seen anyone and then from somewhere to the rear of the cavern emerges a figure that in the light of the sun seems to be a flame with gold so that we are momentarily blinded by the sight. As our eyes become adjusted to this vision, we are astonished for we were expecting to see a Holy Man of great age, but the person that we see is of a Youth of such striking beauty, tall, with skin the colour of Apricot's ripe and in full bloom, Hair of deep chestnut, and eyes oh so tender, and gentle, soft brown, flecked with gold and amber, that seemed to embrace us, with a feeling of utter peace and serenity as if we were known from days long, long ago, before we were even born!

He motioned us to come and sit with him, upon what was a natural seat of rock that went round the whole of the cave, and upon it were cushions of silk, and damask, of velvet and satin, embroidered with flowers and strange emblems that resembled word from a lost civilization.

Our Holy Man sat in the middle and we gathered around him, some of us upon the floor so as to be near to this vision of Light and Spirituality, for that is what radiated from his very being. He talked to us, but the "words" were sounds that we understood and yet they were not of our known world. But they were like food and nectar, we felt refreshed and closed our eyes in rapture and ecstasy.

When we opened them again it was night time, the stars like white sapphires sparkled in the midnight blue of the Heavens, and then as the Moon appeared from behind its canopy of cloud to illumine the sanctuary that we were in, its rays turned everything to Silver and as we looked upon the face of our Holy Man it was as if we were beholding God's own countenance, we were awe struck and speechless. Upon the warm air of the night came the gentle hum of chanting from Monks in a distant monastery, like waves gently breaking upon the shore.

As the Moon's beams played around the Silent figure with arms outstretched in a divine blessing, they seemed to turn into fingers of Silver and Gold light that wrapped themselves around that Holy One, until as the clouds once more faintly obscured the Moons mysterious glow, we found ourselves alone in that cave of solitude! Our vision of the night over were we sad? No! how could we be, when we had been blessed with a blessing that will last forever in our memories and yours little Brother, and yours!!

Our journey, Our Visit, Our Encounter has come to an end We must return! Who was that Divine Being? Who we feel was not of our time or even of our World. All we know is that we have been Privileged for just a little while to be part of something that is unexplainable in Earthly terms but is nevertheless a reality that was unforgettable!

And so little Brother we return your thoughts to you and know that you have, with us, indeed been Blessed.

Farewell dear friend Farewell.